I commend Dr. Carl Herbster and Mr. Ken Howerton for providing this excellent ministry resource for pastors and deacons. Thoughtfully, thoroughly, and biblically written, *Pastor & Deacons* provides highly valuable insight to the men leading today's local churches.

David C. Gibbs III
Christian Law Association

This is a must-read for pastors, pastoral staffs, deacons, and other church leadership. It biblically presents the qualifications and responsibilities of both offices and practically shows how to function together within the church for the glory of God and the edification of the body. I saw these principles practiced effectively while I served as associate pastor of Tri-City for over 30 years. I use this book regularly in training conferences for pastors and church leaders.

Matt Williams
Vice President for Ministry Affairs,
Northland International University

Pastor & Deacons is a must-read for all those in church leadership. I have seen the scriptural principles exemplified in the lives of my pastor, Dr. Carl Herbster and my friend, Ken Howerton. This book is biblical, practical and helpful. It is chock-full of "how to" ideas that will strengthen relationships and promote spiritual unity in the local church. The principles on church discipline and the chapter on "Dealing with Difficulties" are worth the price of the book. Pastor, get this book and you will refer to it often.

Dr. Tom Farrell
Evangelist

Dr. Herbster and Mr. Howerton's book offers insights and practical suggestions for every pastor and deacon who longs to glorify the Lord Jesus Christ. The biblical philosophy presented in this book reminds us of the important pastor/deacon relationship. I am confident this material will be a great help to local churches everywhere.

Paul Chappell
Pastor, Lancaster Baptist Church

I have found *Pastor & Deacons* a wonderful tool to teach the practical aspects and proper relationships of the two church offices we Baptists hold so highly. As Pastor Herbster and Mr. Howerton become transparent with their writing, it becomes obvious that their objective is to share from their hearts what God has allowed them to experience through the years. It is leadership books like this that I find most helpful in my ministry. Any good pastor, deacon, or ministerial student will benefit greatly as he draws from this well of practical wisdom!

Dr. Rick Arrowood
Senior Pastor, Crosspointe Baptist Church
Indianapolis, Indiana

Pastor & Deacons
servants working together

CARL HERBSTER AND
KENNETH HOWERTON

AMBASSADOR INTERNATIONAL
GREENVILLE, SOUTH CAROLINA & BELFAST, NORTHERN IRELAND

www.ambassador-international.com

PASTOR AND DEACONS
Servants Working Together

By Carl Herbster and Kenneth Howerton
Study materials and copy editing by Craig Krueger

Printed in the United States of America

ISBN: 978-1-935507-32-1

Cover Design & Page Layout by David Siglin of A&E Media

AMBASSADOR INTERNATIONAL
Emerald House
427 Wade Hampton Blvd.
Greenville, SC 29609, USA
www.ambassador-international.com

AMBASSADOR BOOKS
The Mount
2 Woodstock Link
Belfast, BT6 8DD, Northern Ireland, UK
www.ambassador-international.com

The colophon is a trademark of Ambassador

TABLE OF CONTENTS

7 The Pastor/Deacon Relationship *109*

The pastor writes about the deacons as his counselors, co-laborers, communicators (those who communicate his intentions and program to any who ask), and close friends. The chairman of the deacons develops seven points, ranging from the fact that the deacons need to understand the pastor's direction and vision for the ministry, to the point that they should not be "yes" men, but honest counselors.

8 The Congregation, Working in Unity *127*

The role of the congregation and their effective work toward the goal of glorifying God through evangelization of the lost and edification of the saints. The unity of the brethren in Acts 8 resulted in the sending of missionaries, the salvation of people, and joy in the city. The case is made for voting as a means of discerning God's will in a group. The role of the church constitution is presented.

9 Let's Talk Finances *141*

Finances will try every ministry, for there is danger and opportunity in both the scarcity and the abundance of money. The principles of stewardship, purpose, giving, and of seeking help are presented. The procedures of budgeting and financial accountability are presented. Loans and debt are discussed.

10 Dealing with Difficulties *157*

Any church will sooner or later face problems with sinful human nature. There will be attacks from within and without. A practical guide to church discipline is developed from Matthew 18. The goal is always restoration.

Appendices *177*

INTRODUCTION

Pastor Carl Herbster has served for over 20 years at Tri-City Baptist Church in Independence, Missouri. Among the many blessings of God in his ministry is an unusually positive and productive working relationship with the deacons of the church. This growing church has started several other churches in the area, has a Christian school, Christian camp (Southland Christian Camp), and is heavily committed to foreign missions.

Mr. Ken Howerton is the kind of layman every pastor hopes to have in his church. A certified program manager with IBM, Ken has served as deacon in two churches (he moved to Missouri from Tennessee), and has been chairman of the deacons in both places. His wisdom and stability, with his commitment to the Lord and His work, have made Ken a gracious servant and wise counselor.

As partners in ministry, these men have also partnered in writing this book. Because each has a unique set of experiences and perspectives, the primary writer of each chapter is identified. It will be helpful to understand the deacon's perspective and the pastor's, not because they are contradictory, but because they are complimentary. The "on-the-job," real-life experience of both men make this a particularly practical book.

—Craig Krueger, Editor

ACKNOWLEDGEMENTS

We would like to thank our wives, Debbie Herbster and Glenda Howerton, for their faithful ministries with us at Tri-City. Both of them play vital roles, not only in our families, but also in the church. Their support and encouragement have been essential to the writing of this book.

We would also like to thank two special friends at Tri-City who have worked very hard on the editing and arranging of this book. Craig Krueger not only has served as a Christian school teacher for over thirty years but also has helped many of us in the ministry to put our thoughts into print. Becky Swisher has been a faithful member of Tri-City for over thirty years and uses her expertise in English to make sure that we produce a manuscript that is free from errors. Without these two wonderful people, this book would not have been possible.

The deacons, staff, and faithful members of Tri-City Baptist Church have given us the wonderful opportunity to serve with them in the work of our Lord and Savior Jesus Christ. Many of the ideas that we share in this book come from our experiences with the good folk at Tri-City. We have experienced many blessings and challenges together. God has directed us as a body into many new ministries, both locally and worldwide. We have watched God do the impossible in bringing us through some difficult situations. As a church family we can truly say together, "We know that all things work together for good to them that love God, to them who are the called according to his purpose" (Romans 8:28).

Pastor Rick Arrowood and Pastor Brad Blanton made valuable contributions to the study questions. We thank these faithful – and thoughtful – pastors for their part in helping people think through and apply these principles for the benefit of many congregations.

Most of all, we thank the Lord Jesus Christ, who has enabled us and has counted us faithful, putting us into the ministry (I Timothy 1:12). Both of us have experienced the business world as well as ministry in the local church. There is no question in either of our minds that the work of the Lord, locally and internationally, is the most important work on earth.

We are thankful that God has allowed us to play a part in His eternal plan to reach the lost and to edify the saints. Our mutual desire and commitment is to remain faithful in His work (I Corinthians 4:2).

—Carl Herbster & Kenneth Howerton

Chapter 1 Carl Herbster

LOCAL CHURCH ORGANIZATION

And I say also unto thee, That thou art Peter, and upon this rock I will build my church; and the gates of hell shall not prevail against it.
Matthew 16:18

God has given me the opportunity to visit hundreds of churches. Some were organized and functioning well, others were not. But whether a church is well-organized or not, if its members are born again, baptized believers who are established on the Word of God, it is God's church. It is God's special property, and its mission is God's special assignment to its members. The Lord Jesus said, "I will build my church." The church is the institution God uses in this age to do His work. The quality and quantity of the work accomplished in a local church will be greatly influenced by how effectively the church is organized. This need for organization is foundational to understanding God's will for the pastor and his deacons.

A TRUE-LIFE EXAMPLE: A CHURCH VOTE AND THE WILL OF GOD[1]

I was excited about the new ministry. Our church was asked to assume leadership of a ministry already bearing much fruit in the Spanish-speaking world. I believed God was leading us into it; the deacons saw it as a special opportunity from the Lord. When the adoption of this ministry was presented for a church vote, 72 per-

---

1 At the beginning of each chapter, an illustration challenges thinking on a biblical principle important to that chapter's topic. Later, the illustration is completed where it fits in the presentation of that principle.

cent voted in favor of it. But 28 percent voted against it. According to the church constitution, a simple majority vote permitted us to proceed. What would you do?

BASIC PRINCIPLES OF ORGANIZATION IN THE LOCAL CHURCH

The Necessity of Teamwork

There is something basic, yet important, that pastors, deacons, and members of a local church can learn from professional football: teamwork. Touchdowns, million-dollar contracts, and crowds of eighty thousand fans motivate a football team to involve each player strategically to accomplish a common goal. When the halfback scrambles for forty yards and scores a touchdown, everyone in the stadium cheers for him. But he did not accomplish this feat alone: offensive guards weighing in at 360 pounds led the way. Without them, the halfback gets squashed! You see, it takes the whole team working together to take a football over the goal line and advance one game closer to the Super Bowl. Surely the local church, with its eternally significant goals should be motivated to involve people as a team in the Lord's work! The church strives to bring people into the kingdom of heaven and then equip them to be involved in God's work—a far higher goal than winning the Super Bowl. Sadly, many local churches fail to work as a team to attain this high goal.

It takes a whole team working together to take a football over the line.

The church at Corinth was a carnal church, plagued with divisions, the opposite of teamwork. In his first letter to the Corinthian church, the apostle Paul rebuked them for this carnality. When they accepted the rebuke and responded to Paul's challenge to do right, problems were resolved. In his second letter, Paul was able to commend them, rather than criticize them. Paul's rebuke had been necessary because the church lacked teamwork and could not attain its goal.

When I coached high school basketball, I would say to my players, "Come on guys! Let's get it together!" That statement captures the heart of effective church organization. It speaks of working together for a common goal without the distraction of interpersonal problems. Paul presents the same idea in I Corinthians 3:9 when he says, "We are labourers together." God does not need us, but He allows us to collaborate with Him if we are willing. He gives us the blessing of seeing our lives, our families, and our churches used for His glory when we enter into the relationship of colaborers with Him. We are on God's team, so to speak, so "let's get it together!"

The Importance of Building Properly

In I Corinthians 3:10, Paul uses the analogy of a building to illustrate the right kind of teamwork: "According to the grace of God which is given unto me, as a wise master builder, I have laid the foundation, and another buildeth thereon. But let every man take heed how he buildeth thereupon." The key word is "how." You must make sure you know how to build the ministry on the foundation. And Who is the cornerstone of the foundation? It is Jesus Christ, the Living Word. This glorious foundation demands a worthy building, so the builder must make sure that he builds properly. He must use the "how-to" manual, the written Word, which reveals the Living Word.

Paul speaks of building upon a foundation in Ephesians 2:18-20, as well: "Through Him we both have access by one Spirit unto the Father. Now therefore ye are no more strangers and foreigners, but fellowcitizens with the saints, and of the household of God; and are built upon the foundation of the apostles and prophets, Jesus Christ Himself being the chief corner stone." How, then, do we build on the cornerstone of the Living Word? How are we fitted together into a building that glorifies God? The instructions are found in the written Word. The same God who saves us and builds us into local churches also gave us the Bible. II Peter 1:21 says, "Holy men of God spake as they were moved by the Holy Ghost." It is the Bible that points men and women to Jesus Christ and then teaches them how to be like Him. The Bible—and only the Bible—is the sufficient guide for building on the foundation of Jesus Christ.

The remainder of I Corinthians 3 discusses building wisely or unwisely. Building materials such as wood, hay, and stubble will burn away at the judgment seat of Christ. Only the gold, silver, and precious stones will remain. How you build matters because the church is the body of

Christ, the temple of the Holy Spirit. Verse 17 says, "If any man defile the temple of God, him shall God destroy; for the temple of God is holy, which temple ye are." God does not want men to defile His church or to destroy it through disunity. In fact, one of the things God hates, according to Proverbs 6, is "he that soweth discord among brethren." God desires His church to be organized and edified, and that is why He gives us such stern warnings to be careful how we build it.

The Value of Order

In chapters 12-14 of I Corinthians, Paul deals with error and confusion regarding the exercise of spiritual gifts. This topic is just as relevant today as the topic of carnal disunity. The proper organization and edification of local churches is seriously hindered by chaos in the worship service. Paul concludes chapter 14 with a statement which applies not only to the exercise of spiritual gifts but also to the whole subject of building a church: "Let all things be done decently and in order" (14:40).

It should not be a surprise that we are given commands about order-liness—we serve an orderly God.

It should not be a surprise that we are given commands about or-derliness—we serve an orderly God. He has the entire universe under control, and nothing is out of place. The sun will come up tomorrow at precisely the right time, and the earth will continue to rotate properly on its axis. Every year the seasons come in the same order. We can count on God to do everything decently and in order. Unfortunately, we cannot always count on people to do everything in the local church decently and in order. That only takes place when people are living biblically.

What is a church? Is it made of bricks and mortar? Is it a campus of buildings? No! The church is people—born again, baptized believers who organize in a community to carry out the work of our Lord and Savior Jesus Christ. "For as the body is one, and hath many members, and all the members of that one body, being many, are one body: so also is Christ. For by one Spirit are we all baptized into one body, whether we be Jews or Gentiles, whether we be bond or free; and have been all made to drink into one Spirit. For the body is not one member, but many" (I Corinthians 12:12-14).

BIBLICAL ROLES FOR ORGANIZATION IN THE LOCAL CHURCH

The Role of the Congregation

When we establish authority in our local churches, we must make certain that God and His people are considered in their proper places. First, we must understand that God has ultimate authority because the church is His special possession, purchased with His own blood (Acts 20:20). Second, we must understand that authority is exercised by the congregation because God, in the Person of the Holy Spirit, indwells the individuals who comprise the congregation. The Holy Spirit first came to indwell believers at Pentecost (Acts 2), and, since that time, part of His ministry has been to indwell people at the moment of salvation. In fact, Romans 8 states that if you do not have the Spirit, you are not God's (Romans 8:9). There is no such thing as a believer who is not indwelt by the Holy Spirit. If God's will is to be accomplished consistently and effectively, the local church must be ruled congregationally because God, the ultimate authority, dwells and works in the individuals of the congregation.

The people (who must all obey God's leadership) are the final authority in the church, not the deacons or even the pastor. The deacons' authority to act is delegated to them by the congregation. Deacons are the servants of the people and the helpers of the pastor, freeing him up for prayer and for the ministry of the Word.

A Bible-believing church should always be seeking to do God's will in God's timing. Decisions about finances, ministries, projects, and programs should be determined by the church as a whole, not by the pastor alone or by a select group of people. When necessary, church votes should be taken so that the membership of baptized believers can determine the will of God for the ministry. We are all at different stages of Christian growth, and none of us perfectly discerns the Spirit's will all of the time. Nonetheless, His will often becomes clear when the whole congregation is seeking it; a general consensus results. Therefore, wise leadership should not move ahead with new plans unless there is much greater agreement than a simple majority. For example, a 90-percent agreement on a particular issue shows the oneness of purpose and spirit that is necessary to keep the unity of the brethren.

Some time ago our church had been asked to assume the leadership of a ministry to the Spanish-speaking world. This was an exciting prospect. We knew the people involved in this ministry to be effective, godly people, whose work showed the blessing of God. The first time this was brought before the membership for a vote, 72 percent voted to take on that ministry. By the rules of the church constitution, that was enough to proceed, but the church leadership thought it would not be wise to go ahead when 28 percent of the people were against the new ministry. They decided to wait, pray, and make more information available. Later, another vote was taken, and 92 percent of the congregation voted for the new ministry. Does that mean that the people who changed their vote were wrong the first time? It really does not matter; the point is, right or wrong, the timing was not right for that ministry to move ahead. With 92 percent in favor of it, the leadership felt that it was not only God's will to proceed, but also God's timing to proceed. The extra time and information made the leadership and the congregation much more confident of the decision and created harmony rather than division.

The Role of the Deacons

As a church grows, the number of ministries, projects, and programs increases. The day-to-day matters of keeping it all functioning become more complicated. There are personnel issues, financial matters, building projects, maintenance work, special needs, educational initiatives, and evangelistic campaigns. These matters would over-burden the average church member if he had to attend to them all. The average person is not able to take the time and effort that all these matters require. The members of the church need help, and the pastoral leaders need help as well. God has a plan for this dilemma. He has determined that there should be special helpers, surrendered servants, who assist the church and the pastor in the ministry details. In Acts we read about God's putting His plan into action and introducing these special servants, the deacons.

And in those days, when the number of the disciples was multiplied, there arose a murmuring of the Grecians against the Hebrews, because their widows were neglected in the daily ministration. Then the twelve called

the multitude of disciples unto them, and said, It is not reason that we should leave the word of God, and serve tables. Wherefore, brethren, look out among you seven men of honest report, full of the Holy Ghost and wisdom, whom we may appoint over this business. But we will give ourselves continually to prayer, and to the ministry of the word.
Acts 6:1-4

The congregation chose qualified servants from among themselves to help the leadership minister effectively to the people. The people chose the deacons, and then the apostles assigned them an area in which to serve. The need to care for widows occasioned the first election of deacons, but the application of the principle to other "business" in the local church is evident.

Rather than exercising authority over the congregation, the deacons exercise authority that is delegated to them by the congregation.

At our church, we do not have a "board" of deacons. You will not find that term in our church constitution; it is something churches have copied from corporate America rather than from the Bible. As we have already noted, God has the ultimate authority in His church, and He leads through the membership of His church. So, contrary to the board structure of a corporation, the decisions are made by the people. Deacons are not equivalent to business executives who call the shots; they are servants of the pastor and the people. They serve the pastor by giving counsel, encouragement, and assistance in meeting the needs of the congregation. They serve the people by attending to details – business details and other kinds – which would be too time consuming for the entire congregation to oversee. Rather than exercising authority over the congregation, the deacons exercise authority that is delegated to them by the congregation.

The deacons receive authority from two sources. First, the church constitution specifies certain matters of business as the responsibility of the deacons. At our church a certain group of deacons has been designated through the constitution to oversee the finances of the church. Other areas of responsibility may be delegated in this manner as well.

Second, the deacons may receive authority through a church vote. When our church relocated facilities, the people of the church did not want to deal with all of the details of drawing up plans, calculating costs, etc. They decided, instead, to put the church's servants to work. They voted to delegate authority to the deacons. The deacons' task was to manage the details of the project and then present plans with an appropriate budget for a congregational vote. When the plans and budget were approved by vote, the people asked the deacons to oversee the actual construction. Again, because the average church member had neither the time nor the expertise to make sure the project was proceeding properly on a daily basis, the deacons were called upon to render their service. Of course, the deacons, in turn, delegated some of their responsibility to the pastor and his staff. Together, the deacons, pastoral staff, and congregation completed the project. Everyone was pleased with the outcome and excited about what God had accomplished through them.

The Role of the Pastor

It is the congregation's responsibility to find a pastor. Many times a congregation will ask its deacons to serve as a pulpit committee, which will then present candidates to the church for a vote. Once the church selects a pastor, he is given authority to function according to the Scriptures, the will of God, and the church constitution. Like the deacons, the pastor also receives authority from the congregation. When our church was seeking a pastor, I was interviewed by the deacons for five hours before being asked to return as a candidate. The following Sunday, the congregation was given the opportunity to ask questions, and after the service there was a fellowship time so that everybody could get to know my family and me. When the vote was taken, the people called me to be their pastor. By their congregational vote, they gave me the authority to feed and oversee the church in accordance with Paul's exhortation to the Ephesian elders: "Take heed therefore unto yourselves, and to all the flock, over the which the Holy Ghost hath made you overseers, to feed the church of God, which he hath purchased with his own blood" (Acts 20:28).

The authority of the pastor is much like the authority which God has given to the man in a Christian home. The husband and father, according to Ephesians 5:23, is to be the spiritual leader in his family. "For the husband is the head of the wife even as Christ is the head of the church." However, with that authority comes heavy responsibility.

If there is a problem with the children, the finances, or the marriage relationship, it is the man's responsibility to solve that problem. It is because of that responsibility that he is given authority to oversee the home. Similarly, the pastor must accept the responsibility for the work of the ministry when he is given the authority to oversee it. He is given the power to perform a task because, in the end, he is accountable for whether the task is done well, done poorly, or not done at all. If there is a problem with the staff, the finances, or relationships, it is the pastor's problem: he must deal with it. Whether dealing with carnality, disorganization, or a lack of discernment, the pastor is responsible to pray, preach, and counsel in a way that seeks to correct the problem.

As a pastor, I am responsible for all the members of this local church and for ministries around the world which are part of our church. I do not take this responsibility lightly. Leading the work of the ministry is a heavy responsibility. Therefore I am thankful God has ordained that special group of servants called deacons to assist in this task. They are wise counselors whose cooperation is essential for church unity. "Where no counsel is, the people fall: but in the multitude of counselors there is safety" (Proverbs 11:14). I do not seek "me" decisions, but "we" decisions. If the deacons and I agree on going a certain direction, it is fairly certain that there will be agreement in the congregational vote as well. On the other hand, when a pastor tries to press ahead without the support of his deacons, he sows the seeds of discord. And when the deacons force the pastor to act against his better judgment, the results are equally disastrous. Unity of mind, unity of spirit, and unity of action are essential for any local church desiring to honor Christ.

If a pastor takes his responsibility seriously, he will see that the pastoral burden is far too heavy for one man. He cannot accomplish alone all that needs to be done in the local church, both at home and on the foreign mission field. In addition to deacons, he must recruit dedicated Christian workers to join him in the ministry. These workers are tremendously valuable to the ministry, whether they are paid staff or volunteers. (Many churches could do without their paid staff before they could afford to lose the godly lay people who faithfully serve.) Many members of our church have given themselves to different ministries. None of the people who put together my radio program are paid; they do it voluntarily. The things they do for the radio ministry would cost thousands of dollars if not for these people.

Both paid staff and volunteers are important, and both are responsible to submit to the authority of the senior pastor. The matter of building such a ministry team is another area where the pastor should seek the counsel of his deacons. However, the pastor must have the freedom to choose his own ministry team just as a coach needs to recruit his own players. When I was considering whether the Lord would have me serve at this church, I asked the deacons, "Am I going to have the right to hire and fire my own staff?" Every pastor should have that authority. If people are going to be on his staff, they must have his philosophy. The pastor is responsible for all those who serve with him, and they are an extension of his work to the people; therefore, he should be empowered to select and train them, whether they are paid staff or volunteers.

Every baptized believer should get involved in some aspect of the ministry.

Even faithful deacons and a pastor with a quality ministry team are not enough to carry out the work of the ministry fully, however. Every born-again, baptized believer in the local church should get involved in some aspect of the ministry. "We are his workmanship created in Christ Jesus unto good works" (Ephesians 2:10). Interestingly, Paul said the primary pastoral role was not doing the ministry, but equipping other believers to do the ministry. God gave pastors to the church for the "perfecting of the saints, for the work of the ministry, for the edifying of the body of Christ" (Ephesians 4:12). In fact, the pastor's staff should help him recruit and train workers with the ultimate goal of getting the whole congregation involved in the work of the ministry. This process can be summarized in five simple, biblical truths:

- The pastors are the equippers (Ephesians 4:12). They recruit and equip people for the work of the ministry.
- The people are the workers (Ephesians 2:10). Everyone needs to be involved somewhere.
- The purpose is Christlikeness (Romans 8:29). "Till we all come… unto the measure of the stature of the fullness of Christ" (Ephesians 4:13).
- The proof is the product in people's lives (II Corinthians 5:17). Are your people becoming more Christlike or more worldly?

- The process is service to God and others (Matthew 20:26-27). The desire for power and authority is the world's way. Jesus taught, "Whosoever of you will be chiefest, shall be servant of all" (Mark 10:44).

The relationships of authority and accountability form an hourglass pattern:

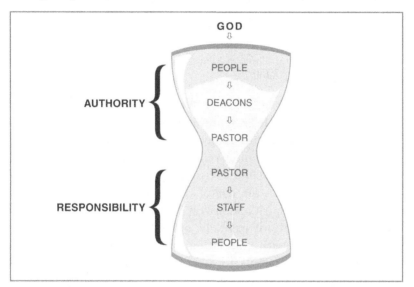

Organizing the Local Church —

I Cor. 14:40: Let all things be done decently and in order.

The authority flows from God through the people — Christians who are indwelt by the Holy Spirit — to deacons, to the pastor. Responsibility flows in almost a reverse pattern: The pastor is responsible for his staff, who are given various ministries in which they are responsible for the people. God is identified above the diagram as being the source of all authority and the One to whom we are all finally responsible.

When Biblical Roles are Distorted

When considering the relationship between the pastoral staff and the deacons, we must be forewarned about some common problems.

Their descriptions can be humorous to read, but they are anything but funny when they happen in a local church. These problems happen because Satan does not want to see the local church succeed. Just as God uses people to build His work, Satan uses people to destroy it. We must avoid the following problems if we want to see God's blessing in our local churches.

Watch out for the Dictator Doctor, the Bombastic Board, Suspicious Saints, the Ambitious Associate, and the Disorganized Organization!

Demanding Dictator

Problem number one is the "Demanding Dictator." This is the pastor who uses his title to win the respect of the people. He uses the Scripture like a hammer to get his way and refuses to seek counsel from the deacons and others in the church. He feels that, as "the Lord's anointed," he has all the answers, and he gives the impression that no one else knows the will of God. The Bible has much to say about such a proud spirit and how it brings contention and destruction. Proverbs 13:10, for example, offers a straightforward rebuke: "Only by pride cometh contention: but with the well advised is wisdom." Pastors are people, too—simply servants of the Lord—and they should avoid with all diligence the know-it-all attitude of the "Demanding Dictator."

Bombastic Board

Problem number two is the "Bombastic Board." Too many times, deacons think of themselves as rulers rather than servants. When that happens, they seek to control the church, when they ought to recognize the authority of the pastor and congregation instead. The pastor could bypass the deacons if he has a "Bombastic Board," but by far the best (and most biblical) way to lead is for the deacons and pastor to seek God's will together and to present their recommendations to the church for a final vote. The deacons should never form a board or control the church behind the scenes. They should always be servants to the people and servants to the pastor. "Bombastic Boards" have frustrated many churches and chased off many pastors; they are never helpful in a local church.

Suspicious Saints

I call problem number three "Suspicious Saints." There always seems to be a group of people who are suspicious of the activities taking place in the church. You hear them say things like, "There's something going on in this church. I can't quite put my finger on it, but there's something wrong here, and I'm going to find it!" God help the church with "Suspicious Saints!" Of course, no church is perfect because its members are only saved sinners, but if a member has a question or concern about anything in the local church, he should address that question or concern specifically to the pastor. No pastor should be afraid of transparency with his people—after all, the people are the final authority. On the other hand, people can promote unity by thinking the best of their pastor and his ministry rather than assuming the worst. Whether it is their premeditated purpose or not, "Suspicious Saints" will spread discord among the brethren. Their questioning and accusing are detrimental to the harmony and unity of any body of believers.

Ambitious Associate

The fourth problem is the "Ambitious Associate." The associate pastor can be a tremendous blessing to a local church and a great help to the senior pastor. But, if the associate pastor's true desire is to be the senior pastor, he will be tempted to undercut the senior pastor's authority. The problematic "Ambitious Associate" may think that if he spreads around enough negativity about the senior pastor, the people will fire the senior pastor and give him the position instead. Desiring to be a senior pastor is not inappropriate, but it is a horrible sin against the church to try to attain that position by destroying someone else's reputation and ministry. The best place for the "Ambitious Associate" is the senior pastorate of another local church where he is free to exercise his gifts. And that will only take place if he receives a recommendation from his senior pastor for having been a supportive and submissive helper. Receive an accusation against an elder only as the Bible prescribes, and even then, make clear to the accuser the seriousness of his accusation. Your first question should be "Have you gone to him alone about this?" (I Timothy 5:19-20, Matthew 18:15-17). Never listen to gossip, especially if it comes from an "Ambitious Associate."

Sad to say, many churches function like a bunch of guys in a sand-lot game.

Disorganized Organization

The fifth problem that can plague the teamwork of the pastor, his staff, and the deacons is the "Disorganized Organization." The local church is supposed to be an organization of believers working together to reach the world with the gospel of Jesus Christ and train disciples. But in many places, not much has changed since Paul had to admonish the church at Corinth to "let all things be done decently and in order" (I Corinthians 14:40). The "Disorganized Organization" creates confusion in our day for people, just as it did in first-century Corinth. We used professional football as an illustration at the beginning of this chapter; perhaps it is appropriate at the end of the chapter as well. Imagine your favorite NFL team choosing and executing plays with no more organization than a bunch of guys in a sand-lot game. As a fan, you would be frustrated, to say the least. Sad to say, many churches function like players in a sand-lot game, not having a proper understanding of procedures for doing God's work.

God will build His church (Matthew 16:18), but He has chosen to do the building through people. Saved, surrendered, and serving people in a local church will be empowered and used by God to expand His work on planet earth. For this work to be accomplished in great quantity and with high quality, the church must be organized.

Spirit-filled people must exercise and delegate authority. The pastor must take the responsibility of making sure the church functions efficiently and effectively. And those special servants we call deacons have the awesome responsibility of helping both pastor and people to fulfill their calling as a local church. We pray this book will help these special servants of the church to work together in unity.

CHAPTER REVIEW

1. The church is God's church, and His Word gives specific instructions for how the church is to be organized.

2. Because the work of the church is of eternal consequence, we should strive to get everyone involved.
3. Disunity defiles God's church.
4. The church must be ruled congregationally because the Holy Spirit makes His will known through the individuals He indwells.
5. The deacons are not a ruling board, but servants of the people and of the pastor.
6. The authority of the deacons is delegated to them by the congregation.

We are on God's team: Let's get it together!

STUDY GUIDES

Discussion group leaders can receive a free Instructor's Annotated Edition of the study guides for each chapter by emailing *info@Tri-City. org*. Please state your position and ministry name (pastor and name of church, seminary or Bible college professor and name of institution, or other discussion group leader) and give a return email address.

GPS (Getting the Principles Summarized)

Find answers to these questions in the chapter.

The Necessity of Teamwork
1. How are a football team and a local church similar? Different?

The Importance of Building Properly
2. What does God hate? (Proverbs 6:19)
3. What attitude is always the cause of conflict in the church – or anywhere else? (Proverbs 13:10)

The Value of Order
4. What is the definition of a local church?
5. What is necessary for "people to do everything in the local church decently and in order"?

The Role of the Congregation
6. Who is (or are) the final authority (or authorities) for decision making in the local church?

The Role of the Deacons
7. What chapter in the Bible tells about the beginning of deacons in the church? What three qualities describe these people? As those first deacons took care of that time's current need, what did they free up the apostles to do?
8. Who chose the first deacons, and who assigned them a task to do?
9. Whom do the deacons serve?

Role of the Pastor
10. Whose responsibility is it to select a pastor for the local church? How, then, may deacons become involved.
11. What does Acts 20:28 say about the source of authority for the local church pastor? What two categories of responsibility are listed?

 APPles (Applying the Principles Practically)

Apply these ideas to your church. Discussion will often go beyond just the facts in the reading.

The Importance of Building Properly
1. If "contention" only comes by pride (Proverbs 13:10), how is that true when a person contends for non-negotiable biblical principles, for example, the appointment of a female pastor?

The Value of Order
2. Paraphrase I Corinthians 14:40.
(In a paraphrase, do not use any of the main words from the original. This helps you to think through the meaning. Bible study tools are allowed, but do not simply copy another translation.)

The Role of the Congregation

3. Discuss the difference between who has "ultimate authority" in the church and who makes the decisions.

4. Why are not the deacons or the pastor the final authority for decisions in the church? That is, defend the practice of congregational rule.

The Role of the Deacons

5. What is the difference between a church having a board and a church having deacons?

The Role of the Pastor

6. Is it true that every problem in the church is the pastor's problem? Defend your answer.

7. Discuss the idea of "we" decisions as superior to "me" decisions.

8. What if, after the decision is made, you still believe the "other idea" was better?

When Biblical Roles are Distorted

9. Choose one of the five problem categories presented at the end of chapter 1. From your experience (avoid identifying individuals) or in a realistic theoretical case, explain how you would deal with the matter from your role as pastor or deacon.

THE SERVANT LEADER

After he had washed their feet, and had taken his garments, and was set down again, he said unto them, Know ye what I have done to you? ... If I then, your Lord and Master, have washed your feet; ye also ought to wash one another's feet. ... If ye know these things, happy are ye if ye do them.
John 13:12, 14, 17

The deacons of any church are not a governing board. The office, as it is defined in Scripture, is one of a servant: a servant to the pastor, to the church, and, most of all, to the Lord.

When it is time to elect deacons, I, as a layman in the church, am going to nominate people that I believe have a servant's attitude. When I have served as chairman of our deacons, I have also had the opportunity to interview men who have been nominated as deacons. In explaining the requirements of the office, I encourage them to become deacons for the purpose of serving. If the people of your church have elected you as a deacon, their choice should have been based on their seeing that servant's spirit in you. People can only look on the outside; only God looks on the heart. You, as a deacon, know whether you have this servant's attitude. At our best, all of us have room to grow in this area. We must develop a servant's attitude if we are to earn the Lord's "well done" for our service as deacons.

A TRUE-LIFE EXAMPLE: THE SECRET AGENDA OF THE STEALTH DEACONS

We could not have seen it coming. A certain church in my past was flourishing. The church had just come out of a compromising religious group, and God was blessing abundantly. But a few people did not like the new direction. What would happen if they contrived to get on the church board with the hidden agenda of bringing the church back into the former group?

IF THE LORD JESUS WERE A DEACON: THE EXAMPLE OF CHRIST AS SERVANT

The Attitude of a Servant

The servant is others-oriented. After the Last Supper the Lord caught His disciples completely by surprise, and the Holy Spirit reinforces that sense of surprise for us in the way that event was recorded:

> *Now before the feast of the Passover, when Jesus knew that his hour was come that he should depart out of this world unto the Father, having loved his own which were in the world, he loved them unto the end. And supper being ended, the devil having now put into the heart of Judas Iscariot, Simon's son, to betray him; Jesus knowing that the Father had given all things into his hands, and that he was come from God, and went to God; He riseth from supper, and laid aside his garments; and took a towel and girded himself. After that he poureth water into a bason, and began to wash the disciples' feet. . . .*
> John 13:1-5

What a picture! We would expect it to have been all about Jesus on that night. He was the master. He was the beloved leader. He was the one betrayed. He was the one facing the most difficult time of His life and the very crisis on which all history turns. But for Him, the focus was on others. He took the most humble role and illustrated servant leadership to eleven disciples. Yes, Jesus washed their feet, but He was really concerned about equipping them with one of the essential attitudes for successful service and the rewards that follow.

The servant is not self-centered. Focus on one's own way is the opposite of the "others-centered" attitude. Controlling the natural desire to get your own way is essential to effectively serving. If you will be the Lord's follower as a deacon, the same must be true for you. It is not about you; it is about honoring the Lord by serving. It is not about your schedule or whether you get respect or whether your ideas are most listened-to; it is all about how you can serve.

The servant attitude says, "I don't want my will or my desires; I want your desires, God."

The deacon does not work with a hidden goal or a personal agenda. He does not think, "If I could be a deacon, I could make this certain thing happen" —unless, of course, it is a matter of clear biblical principle. You do not want to become a deacon with the wrong attitude. You should become a deacon to serve the people, your fellow deacons, your pastor, and the Lord. Do not come with a desire to get your own way. That would be a selfish attitude, not a servant attitude. The servant attitude says, "I don't want my will or my desires; I want your desires, God. I want to serve You with all my heart. I want to be the best deacon I can be. I want the decisions we make as deacons to be Your decisions. I want to always have the attitude of serving the body of believers." This attitude will please the Lord.

In one church where I was a deacon, there was a rotating deacon board. Each year three men would rotate off the board after their three-year term of service was completed, and three other men were elected. The church had just come out of a compromising religious group, but there were a few men who wanted to take the church back into it. The deacon board was made up of twelve men. Therefore, six men got together, plotted, and positioned themselves to be elected as deacons. They went out and mustered up enough support to make this happen. It took two years—one year to get three men on, one more year to get the next three in place.

When they were positioned, things began to happen. Shortly after the second election, they asked the pastor to resign, and they took the church back into the other group. They accomplished their secret agenda, but that was not all that happened. Prior to this plotting process, the church was averaging 1200 in Sunday school. After these deacons began to execute their plot, there was a church split. Many people left the church, and the ministry began to go down. The attendance went down to about 300. The debt load of the church became a burden to those 300 people. They have struggled for many years and still struggle with this debt and other problems.

This all happened because of deacons with a self-centered motive. These deacons had not allowed the Lord to put His goals into their hearts. They had predetermined their own goals and had premeditated their own plans. I think the Lord will judge that kind of character and attitude in a direct way. As a deacon, I would be fearful of doing something like that in the church. Let me encourage you to have the attitude of being a servant—not a dictator, not a ruler, not a self-directed individual who carries his own personal goals into the office of deacon, saying, "I'm going to get this accomplished." Kill that attitude and say, "Lord, I want to get done what You want accomplished. I want Your mind." Then you will be successful, and then you will please the Lord.

One final thought on being others-centered: the servant does not have to be appreciated by people. The greatest incident of lack of appreciation is Judas' betrayal of the Lord of Glory. For thirty pieces of silver, perhaps the price of a slave, Judas betrayed the One who loved even him, the betrayer. The greatest test of your servant spirit comes when you are treated as a servant.

The servant is humble. The Lord took a towel and a basin and performed a lowly service, dirty work, work not fitting for a man of his station in life.

How small a thing it is to "rejoice with them that do rejoice, and weep with them that weep" (Romans 12:15). Here I think of one deacon in particular. Norman has a great sense of the importance of the church as a family. If there is a wedding or if there is a funeral, Norman and his wife are there. Even if, in this large church, he is not especially close to the families involved, they are still part of our church family, and Norman wants to honor and encourage them.

We as deacons must grow enough to be humble. Small-minded people cannot grace humble work with the earnest diligence that makes those tasks to be sacrifices of worship. Can you mow your pastor's lawn or set up chairs for Sunday school with the same enthusiasm with which you would present a major building plan before the church?

The servant is also persuasive. Peter was not ready for this turn of events:

Peter saith unto him, Lord, dost thou wash my feet?

Jesus answered and said unto him, What I do thou knowest not now; but thou shalt know hereafter. Peter saith unto him, Thou shalt never wash my feet. Jesus answered him, If I wash thee not, thou hast no

part with me. Simon Peter saith unto him, Lord, not my feet only,
but also my hands and my head.
John 13:6-9

Peter did not want to accept this humble service. He loved and respected the Lord, and this foot-washing did not fit Peter's idea of what was appropriate. But the Lord knew just how to convince Peter to accept His service.

Sometimes the deacon's role may involve persuading people – whether pastors, widows, or others – to accept their help. Too many, especially men, are "Lone Rangers," reluctant to accept help. This persuasion requires great wisdom, tact, and timing.

The art of persuasion is, in part, the art of listening. One of my fellow deacons is a master of this art. In our meetings, we have adapted a line from the E. F. Hutton ad: "When Paul talks, people listen." As the deacons and the pastor exchange ideas, Paul listens and evaluates. Some of us are quick to venture out; some are more cautious. Our different spiritual gifts, such as gifts of teaching, helps, mercy, or administration allow us to see an issue from different angles. Through it all, Paul is thoughtfully listening. Finally, when Paul offers his insights or evaluation, his words command special attention, not because he has been silent through most of the discussion, but because we know he has been taking it all in and prayerfully evaluating.

Not all persuasiveness is good. There is a difference between the deacon's persuasively offering help and his insistence on having his own way. We want to serve God by serving the pastor and the people, but insisting on "winning" by getting one's own way is still pride—the root of all sin.

The Burden of a Servant

Consider Christ, our example, praying in the Garden just prior to His appointed hour. He asked God the Father for the burden of the cross to be lifted from Him, but pleasing God was more important than anything else, even the suffering which He knew that He would endure. This burden was so great that His sweat became like great drops of blood. But praise God this "servant" accomplished the work that He was sent to do. Our burden will never be as heavy as the burden Jesus bore for us.

We also see that Jesus cared for others, not only in meeting spiritual needs, but also in meeting physical needs. He especially expressed his care for His mother when He asked John to make sure that his mother's needs would be met (John 19:27). Let us, as deacons, bear our burdens willingly and meet the needs of people as our Lord did.

The Reward of a Servant

Recognition of a job completed, a mission accomplished—these are the rewards of the Master to his servant.

"Well done, thou good and faithful servant . . . enter thou into the joy of thy lord" (Matthew 25:21, 23). This was the reward to the servants who had used well the talents given to them. God has given each of us gifts and abilities to be used in His service. In serving as deacons, we have a special opportunity to use the talents which God has given to us for His glory.

Because of his faithfulness in defending the faith, the first deacon was martyred, but God gave him a glimpse of Heaven just before he died. He was able to see the glory of God and Jesus standing on the right hand of God (Acts 7:55). What a reward!

The Accountability as a Servant: A Visual Reminder

In order to maintain this servant's attitude, it is the responsibility of the deacons and pastor to encourage each other and to hold each other accountable. To this end, I offer the following practical suggestion.

He who dies with the dirtiest towel wins.

At the beginning of the year, bring to the deacons meeting a towel which will serve as a symbol of servanthood (John 13:5). The world's materialism is summarized in the slogan, "He who dies with the most toys wins." The towel with which the Lord girded himself when He washed the disciples' feet suggests another idea: "He that has the dirtiest towel wins." Call the towel the "Servant's Towel." Have the towel embroidered with your church's name and the words "Servant's Towel." At the bottom of the towel, put the words "Model the way for someone today", or use Scripture, "Let your light so shine," or "Be thou an example of the believers."

The chairman can choose the first Servant of the Month. The recipient of the servant award will choose the recipient for the next month. All the deacons are challenged to look for occasions when they see other deacons serving. Challenge the deacons to "model the way for someone today." Set aside a time in the deacons meeting to honor the chosen Servant of the Month. Use this time to encourage that deacon—to demonstrate to him that you see him serving, that you appreciate his servant's heart. This will go a long way in holding each other accountable with a very positive tone. It is a way to "inspect what you expect." For some reason, probably because of our sin nature, thing we expect do not seem to happen unless we have some kind of follow-up. Do not expect something unless you inspect it. Do not display this towel in the church or put it on the bulletin board. Keep it within the deacon organization. We are not seeking recognition. We are just seeking to serve the Lord and to have a means of accountability.

This is certainly in line with the Holy Spirit's work in our lives. As we do things, or fail to do things, the Holy Spirit is the inspector, trainer, and motivator of our lives. This is just one way that you can challenge and encourage one another to focus upon servanthood.

HOW TO PLAY SECOND FIDDLE

A Devotional Presented at a Meeting of the Deacons by Mike Stephenson, Deacon

An admirer once asked the famous orchestra conductor Leonard Bernstein what was the most difficult instrument to play. He responded with quick wit: "Second fiddle. I can get plenty of first violinists, but to find one who plays second violin with as much enthusiasm or second French horn or second flute, now that's a problem. And yet if no one plays second, we have no harmony."

As deacons, we are a support team to everyone else. We are not the rulers of all, but the servants of all. This role can sometimes be difficult, one that goes against our nature. The desire to be number one is not a new problem:

Then came to him the mother of Zebedee's children with her sons, worshipping him, and desiring a certain thing of him. And he said unto

her, What wilt thou? She saith unto him, Grant that these my two sons may sit, the one on thy right hand, and the other on the left, in thy kingdom. But Jesus answered and said, Ye know not what ye ask. Are ye able to drink of the cup that I shall drink of, and to be baptized with the baptism that I am baptized with? They say unto him, We are able. And he saith unto them, Ye shall drink indeed of my cup, and be baptized with the baptism that I am baptized with: but to sit on my right hand, and on my left, is not mine to give, but it shall be given to them for whom it is prepared of my Father. And when the ten heard it, they were moved with indignation against the two brethren. But Jesus called them unto him, and said, Ye know that the princes of the Gentiles exercise dominion over them, and they that are great exercise authority upon them. But it shall not be so among you: but whosoever will be great among you, let him be your minister; And whosoever will be chief among you, let him be your servant.
Matthew 20:20-27

It's not easy playing "second fiddle." Our society is geared to the achiever climbing the corporate ladder, to building self-esteem, to improving our self-image, and to other vain pursuits that expose our desire to be "first violin." Jesus stated in Matthew 20:28, "The Son of man came not to be ministered unto, but to minister, and to give his life a ransom for many." He was our example of a servant. The Son of God, Creator of the universe, King of kings, and Lord of lords came to serve, not to be served. How much more should we serve others.

Deacon comes from the Greek word *diakonos* (dee-ak-on-os), meaning "to be an attendant, i.e. wait upon (menially) or as a host or a friend; minister unto, serve, use the office of a deacon." Our position as deacons is not to call attention to ourselves, but to minister to others, specifically, to the pastor, to the church, to the widows, and to each other. My son John plays the violin. I have not learned much from his violin lessons, but I know that to play a good second fiddle requires several steps.

Proper Instrument

If we do not have the proper instrument, the quality is not as good. Usually, the proper instrument is not a new instrument. When we were searching for a violin for my son, we were told by his teacher, "Do not buy a new instrument." The ones that have been "proved" are the best.

We are told in I Timothy 3:10, "And let these also first be proved; then let them use the office of a deacon, being found blameless."

Proper Tuning

After we have selected the proper instrument, the next step is to properly tune that instrument. If the violin is out of tune, it is of little good to anyone. Likewise, if our hearts are out of tune, we cannot be effectively used by God and are of little value in His service. We are told in Proverbs 4:23 to "keep thy heart with all diligence; for out of it are the issues of life." Also, Proverbs 23:7a says, "For as he thinketh in his heart, so is he." Matthew 5:8 states, "Blessed are the pure in heart: for they shall see God." As we can see, God admonishes us to have pure hearts, hearts that are kept "in tune."

Practice

Practice is the basis of everything that is done well. Talent does not substitute for practice. Even the greatest musician must devote his life to practice to be able to use the talent God has given him. In our Christian life, to be a Christian is not enough; we have to practice being a Christian. God told the children of Israel in Leviticus 20:8, "And you shall keep my statutes and do them." It was not enough to have His statutes. They had to put them into practice. They had to "keep . . . and do" them. Ezra 7:10 says, "For Ezra had prepared his heart to seek the law of the Lord, and to do it, and to teach in Israel statutes and judgments." Psalms 106:3 states, "Blessed are they that keep judgment, and he that doeth righteousness at all times!" Great musicians would not think of performing without practicing. How much more should we "practice" to be able to serve the Lord Jesus Christ.

Proper First-violin Tuning

Several weeks ago my son John was playing second violin in a group, and the person playing first violin was slightly out of tune. Even though only slightly out of tune, the first violinist caused the second violins to play out of tune. We have to make sure the leaders we select are properly "in tune," or they can cause us to stray from the truth and from the will of God. This is exactly what happened when God told the children of Israel to go and possess the land of Canaan. In Numbers 13:2-3 God said, "Send thou men, that they may search the land of

Canaan, which I give unto the children of Israel: of every tribe of their fathers shall ye send a man, every one a ruler among them. And Moses by the commandment of the Lord sent them from the wilderness of Paran: all those men were heads of the children of Israel."

Not all of the leaders that were chosen were in tune with God. Numbers 13:31-32 shows the result: "But the men that went up with him said, We are not able to go up against the people, for they are stronger than we. So they brought up an evil report of the land which they had searched unto the children of Israel, saying, The land, through which we have gone to search it, is a land that eateth up the inhabitants thereof; and all the people that we saw in it are men of great stature." But two of the leaders were in tune with God, as we find out in Numbers 14:6-9: "And Joshua the son of Nun, and Caleb the son of Jephunneh, which were of them that searched the land, rent their clothes; and they spake unto all the company of the children of Israel, saying, The land, which we passed through to search it, is an exceedingly good land. If the Lord delight in us, then he will bring us into this land, and give it us; a land which floweth with milk and honey. Only rebel not ye against the Lord; neither fear ye the people of the land; for they are bread for us; their defense is departed from them, and the Lord is with us: fear them not." That faith-based exhortation is leadership in tune! You cannot play the proper second fiddle if you do not have leadership that is "in tune."

Our responsibility, then, is to pray for one another, to encourage one another, and, if necessary, to appropriately confront and exhort one another to keep our hearts in tune with God.

Performance

Performance is the goal. This is not performance in the sense of an unreal act, like actors on a stage. A musical performance brings the silent, written score into the full reality that the composer designed.

God intended for us not just to possess, but also to perform. Consider these words:

- Leviticus 18:4 : "Ye shall do my judgments, and keep my ordinances, to walk therein; I am the Lord your God."
- Deuteronomy 4:14 : "And the Lord commanded me at that time to teach you statutes and judgments, that ye might do them in the land whither ye go over to possess it."

- Psalms 119:112 : "I have inclined mine heart to perform thy statutes alway, even unto the end."

Playing second fiddle may not seem very important or attractive, but that is where the blessing is—if you have prepared and practiced and performed to the level that God has for you. Without the role of second fiddle, beautiful harmony cannot be achieved. The conclusion of the matter is found in I Corinthians 9:19, where Paul says, "For though I be free from all men, yet have I made myself servant unto all, that I might gain the more."

CHAPTER REVIEW

1. Deacons are not rulers of the church, but servant leaders.
2. The servant is not self-centered, but others-centered.
3. The deacon knows which gifts God has given him for service, and he humbly uses them.
4. Sometimes the deacon must find ways to persuade people to let him help them, but he must be sure that he is helping them and not advancing himself.
5. To be a help to others, to play "second fiddle" exquisitely, requires:
6. The proper instrument.
7. Proper tuning.
8. Practice.
9. Proper first-violin tuning.
10. Performance.

Be great: Serve!

STUDY GUIDE

 GPS (Getting the Principles Summarized)

Find answers to these questions in the chapter.

The Attitude of a Servant
1. Why did Christ wash the disciples' feet?
2. What attitudes are listed in contrast to a servant's spirit?
3. What is "the greatest test of your servant spirit"?

How to Play Second Fiddle
4. What is the Greek word for deacon, and what does it mean?

Proper First-violin Tuning
5. What happens if a leader is out of tune?

 APPles (Applying the Principles Practically)

Apply these ideas to your church. Discussion will often go beyond just the facts in the reading.

The Attitude of a Servant
1. Explain the balance of humility and persuasiveness.

The Burden of a Servant
2. How can you keep from burn-out and frustration as you carry the responsibilities of your role as pastor or deacon?

The Accountability as a Servant
3. Discuss the pro's and con's of the monthly "Servant's Towel" award.

Practice
4. How does the practice principle apply to the work of a pastor or deacon?

Proper First-violin Tuning
5. Since having a leader (first violin) out of tune is bad for all, how is that problem remedied?

THE OFFICE AND QUALIFICATIONS OF THE PASTOR

If a man desire the office of a bishop, he desireth a good work.
I Timothy 3:1

In the Apostle Paul's mind, local church ministries were far too important to wait for his arrival. He explained to Timothy why he was writing: "These things write I unto thee, hoping to come unto thee shortly: But if I tarry long, that thou mayest know how thou oughtest to behave thyself in the house of God, which is the church of the living God" (I Timothy 3:14-15). Paul knew that his visit might be delayed or might not take place at all, and it was imperative for Timothy to have instructions which he could implement in the church regardless of Paul's itinerary. In these instructions we find practical teaching on the offices and qualifications of pastors and deacons. This teaching is obviously foundational to the subject of the pastor/deacon relationship, so it is necessary that we review it briefly, beginning with the office and qualifications of a pastor.

A TRUE-TO-LIFE APPLICATION: CLEAR CHOICES, NOT EASY CHOICES[2]

It is not unusual for my phone to ring in the middle of the night, and I really do not mind. If my people are hurting, I am hurting with them. But there is a particular stab of pain in my soul when I hear the voice of another full-time Christian worker on the other end. This par-

---

2 "True-to-Life" illustrations are based on one or more real situations, but are thoroughly fictionalized to protect identities.

ticular night, it was a pastor friend in another state. I had long known that he was concerned about his children's increasingly sour attitude toward anything spiritual, but the point of crisis had finally come. There were no easy, behind-the-scenes options left. What clear direction could the Word of God give him? And what would be the result if he risked all on obedience to that direction?

THE OFFICE OF A PASTOR

Biblical Words for the Pastor

Before we proceed, we must answer a basic question about the number of local church offices. Are there only two offices, or are there more? Some people believe that the church should be led by bishops and elders as well as by pastors and deacons. There are many variations on this idea, and some churches have a more complex hierarchy than others, but the biblical model is not complicated. In I Timothy, a letter devoted to local church matters, only two offices are named.

> *The terms pastor, elder, and bishop (also translated overseer in the King James Version) . . . are all used interchangeably.*

In naming only two offices, I Timothy agrees with the rest of the New Testament. Although the New Testament uses the terms "pastor," "elder," and "bishop" (also translated "overseer" in the King James Version), the three terms are used interchangeably. Consider Acts 20:17-38 where Luke records Paul's farewell address to the leaders of the Ephesian church. In verse 17 Luke referred to the leaders as elders, but Paul's word for them in verse 28 is "overseers," (which is the same word as "bishops" in the Greek). For those who believe in the inerrancy of Scripture, the only logical explanation is that the terms "elders" and "bishops" ("overseers") are synonymous since they refer to one group of men. In I Peter 5:1-2, we find a similar use of two terms to describe one group of men. Peter instructs the elders to "feed the flock," an expression which is one word in the original language. That one word, "poimaino," is the verb form of the noun "pastor." In other words, the elders are instructed to pastor the flock, which signifies that "elders" and "pastors" refer to the same office. When we carefully consider Acts 20, I Peter 5, and similar passages, we must conclude that there are only two offices, pastor and deacon, and that the office of pastor can be described by three terms. Rather than referring to three separate offices, these three terms emphasize various facets of the pastoral ministry. While "pastor" indicates the shepherding role, meeting the needs of those in his care, "elder" refers to the required maturity, and "bishop" signifies the leader's ultimate responsibility to God as overseer, or supervisor, for all that happens in the church.

The Foundation of the Apostles and Prophets

Ephesians 4:11-12 says, "He gave some, apostles; and some, prophets; and some, evangelists; and some, pastors and teachers: For the perfecting of the saints, for the work of the ministry, for the edifying of the body of Christ." According to Ephesians 2:20, two of these offices, the apostles and prophets, formed the foundation of the church. They were the "holy men of God" used to pen the New Testament Scriptures (II Peter 1:21). These offices no longer function, since their foundational role has been fulfilled.

The Continuing Ministry of Evangelists and Pastors

The other two offices named in Ephesians 4:11-12 have a continuing ministry. In the New Testament, an evangelist was sent out by a local church—and I believe that pattern should continue—but his ministry is not limited to one particular church. Strictly speaking, the evangelist does not hold a local church office. He functions within many local churches, reaching the masses with the gospel and sometimes planting new churches as well. The pastor, on the other hand, ministers in one local church. We first read about pastors in Acts 14:23: "And when they had ordained them elders in every church, and prayed with fasting, they commended them to the Lord, on whom they believed." After the churches were established by church-planting evangelists, pastors were placed in authority in each local assembly. They were entrusted with the continuing task of nurturing and discipling believers, as our Lord commanded in the Great Commission (Matthew 28:19-20). Of course, the pastor will be a soulwinner, too. In fact, he must lead the way and model this, since he must be an example of any of the disciplines of the Christian life.

In the first churches, these pastors were appointed by the church planters, and this is still sometimes done today. In most established churches, however, the congregation chooses a pastor. The newly chosen pastor will continue serving in that capacity as long as both he and the congregation believe it is God's will for him to remain.

A church with multiple heads is no more natural than a two-headed person.

After reading Acts, it is fair to ask if there ought to be a plurality of elders/pastors/bishops in the local church. The Bible neither commands nor forbids a plurality of elders, and many larger churches will have many men serving on the pastoral staff. In any effective organization, however, there can be only one head. Ultimately, one man must be responsible for the ministry, and that is the real issue when we discuss the "plurality of elders." Some seem to think the ministry should be led by committee, so to speak, but a church with multiple heads is no more natural than a two-headed person walking down the street. I think it is instructive that the letters to the churches in the book of Revelation address only one "angel" in each church. The word "angel" is also translated "messenger," and is usually interpreted as meaning, in Revelation 1:20-3:22, the human pastor, rather than a supernatural being. The Spirit does not address the "angels" (plural) of the Church at Ephesus or the "angels" of the church at Laodicea. In each church there was one messenger, one man who was accountable for shepherding the church on behalf of the Chief Shepherd, Jesus Christ.

THE QUALIFICATIONS OF A PASTOR

In I Timothy, Paul makes it clear that only a certain kind of man may be a pastor. This text supplies a list of qualifications:

A bishop, then, must be blameless, the husband of one wife, vigilant, sober, of good behaviour, given to hospitality, apt to teach, Not given to wine, no striker, not greedy of filthy lucre; but patient, not a brawler, not covetous; One that ruleth well his own house, having his children in subjection with all gravity; (For if a man know not how to rule his own house, how shall he take care of the church of God?) Not a novice, lest being lifted up with pride he fall into the

*condemnation of the devil. Moreover he must have a good report
of them which are without; lest he fall into reproach and the snare
of the devil.*
I Timothy 3:2-7

A man who desires to be a pastor must have a good testimony; he
must possess godly character; he must have the ability to minister effectively; and he must have a family that is a model for other Christian
families. Church members must carefully consider these characteristics before they call a man to be the shepherd of their local assembly.

A Good Testimony

The first and last qualifications listed by Paul relate to the pastor's
testimony. He must be blameless or "above reproach" (verse 2). Because
he represents the local church, he must also "have a good report of
them which are without" (verse 7); that is, he must have a good reputation in the community at large, not just in the church. If he is to have
a positive impact on people outside the church as well as within the
church, a positive testimony is absolutely essential.

A Godly Personal Character

Many qualifications are given in I Timothy 3 relating to the pastor's possessing godly personal character. He must be "vigilant, sober, of
good behaviour, given to hospitality . . . not given to wine, no striker,
not greedy of filthy lucre; but patient, not a brawler, not covetous." He
is to be known as a man of virtue.

An Ability to Minister Effectively

Two phrases in Paul's list indicate that a pastor must be equipped
for the job: "apt to teach" and "not a novice." He must be able to
teach because teaching is a major ingredient in the pastoral ministry.
When Paul says that the pastor cannot be a novice, he is requiring a
certain degree of spiritual maturity and experience. A new believer
is simply not able to shepherd the flock effectively; he needs time to
grow and to acquire wisdom that only comes with spiritual maturity
and experience.

A Model Christian Family

The family qualifications of a pastor deserve special attention because they are vital qualifications that are under constant attack. These prerequisites can even be controversial among Christians. The first family qualification is directly related to the pastor's testimony, and it is probably the most controversial in the entire list. Paul states that a pastor must be the husband of one wife. The word "husband" is at the center of the first controversy we must address. That word, of course, means that only a man may be a pastor. Some people object to this, but the Bible is unmistakable on this point. If we accept the Bible, there is only one position for us to take. In our day, some people teach that women can be pastors, but restricting the office to men is perfectly consistent with other Scriptures relating to the roles of men and women in the church. First Timothy 2:12, for example, is crystal clear: "I suffer not a woman to teach, nor to usurp authority over the man." Since pastoral work includes both teaching and exercising authority over men, women are not biblically permitted to be pastors.

The word "husband" also raises the question of whether a pastor must be a married man. Some believe that it is mandatory for pastors to be married; others believe that single men may also be qualified. It seems obvious, however, that a single man is not the husband of one wife. Besides plain interpretation, there are good practical reasons for taking this position. A godly wife serving alongside a committed man is a dynamic relationship for church ministry. And a godly pastor's wife certainly gives her husband invaluable experience and advice in dealing with women in the local church. It goes without saying that a pastor's wife is uniquely equipped to teach and serve in women's ministries as well.

The words "one wife" are at the center of another controversy we must address. Paul unequivocally requires that a pastor be the husband of one, and only one, wife. How does this apply to divorce and remarriage? Numerous books have been written on the topic, and they raise a legitimate question. Should a candidate for pastoral ministry be accepted if he has ever been divorced? I believe a man who is married and has never been divorced best fulfills the requirement "husband of one wife" as well as the qualification of a good testimony.

The home is extremely important to our Lord. How can a man lead the church if his own home is a mess?

In I Timothy 3:4-5, Paul lays down another family qualification for a pastor. He is to be "one that ruleth well his own house, having his children in subjection with all gravity; (For if a man know not how to rule his own house, how shall he take care of the church of God?)" The home is extremely important to our Lord; it is the first institution that He established, and it is the basic institution upon which all others are built. It must, therefore, be a priority of the local church to build strong families. How can a man lead the church in pursuing that priority if his own home is a mess? It is essential that a pastor be one who trains his children according to the Word of God. His children are sinful human beings like anyone else's children; they will not always do right. But they ought to demonstrate a basic pattern of obedience and be growing in respect for authority. To put it another way, the pastor's children need not be perfect, but they must be in the *process of becoming* more like Christ. The pastor's home should be an illustration to the rest of the church and to the community. Churches must be careful to evaluate the characteristics not only of the pastor himself, but also of the pastor's wife and children. Sad to say, too many pastors' homes have been a disgrace in the church and in the community.

I knew why my friend and fellow pastor was staring down into his coffee. I have been through this scene, with variations, many times. If he looked up, I would see the tears that were beginning to form in his eyes. At his request, I had driven across two states to meet him at this restaurant and talk about his family. His teenage children had gone past stubborn attitudes to rebellious actions that no one could miss, especially the members of his church. Curfews were ignored, as were admonitions about wrong friends. The fifteen-year-old daughter would sit in the back row at church with her arms crossed and her head sullenly down. The seventeen-year-old son did not even bother coming to church anymore. It was no longer a gray area; he clearly did not qualify as "one that ruleth well his own house, having his children in subjection with all gravity." We both knew what he had to do, but it hurt, and it propelled his family into uncertainty. Yet this was a simple matter of obedience to the Word of God, and he would have to trust God for the results.

He first met with his family. He confessed specific failures as the leader of his home and asked them to forgive him. Then he met with the deacons to tell them what he had decided to do and why. In the next Sunday evening service he stood before his people and explained that he no longer met the I Timothy 3 requirements for a pastor and would have to resign from the pastorate.

It took two years and a move to another state, but God blessed. He got a secular job, but he was careful to take a job that did not keep him away from his family excessively. He worked to balance love and firm discipline. He won his children by the steady investment of love, time, and talk. They were first skeptical, then sobered by the results of their own self-centeredness, and finally convicted of their sin by the Holy Spirit. They got right with God and with their parents. After two years, the son was a freshman in a Christian college, and the daughter was a vibrant leader in her youth group.

No action that one person takes can guarantee a certain response from someone else, but in my experiences so far, this has been the result 100% of the time. When men have tried to hang on to their positions as pastors while attempting to rescue their children, there is a lower success rate. I believe that the difference lies both in the following of Scriptural principles and in the sobering effect on the children when they realize the results of their attitudes and actions.

One more note on helping your pastor's children be all they can be: Do not tell them to be good "because you're the pastor's kids." First, the pastor's children have the same reason to do right that everyone else—child or adult—has. "Let your light so shine before men, that they may see your good works, and glorify your Father which is in heaven." Second, making a child believe that he is held to a different standard just because his father is a pastor can make that child resent the fact that his father is a pastor. There is a place for the pastor himself to explain to his children their potential to affect his ministry, but this should not be a bargaining chip for discipline.

In the business world much time and effort are given to the interviewing of a potential employee. The potential employee wants to know what will be expected of him or her, and the employer wants to know if the person under consideration is qualified for the job. How much more important is the process of interviewing a man for the position of pastor! Since "everything rises and falls on leadership," every church must take the office and qualifications of a pastor seriously.

CHAPTER REVIEW

1. The Bible prescribes two current offices in the local church: pastor and deacon.
2. As pastor, he shepherds; as elder, he is mature; as bishop, he administrates.
3. The evangelist serves in many local churches winning souls and planting new churches.
4. The pastor serves in one local church nurturing and discipling—but he also models the soulwinning expected of all believers.
5. In any effective organization, there can only be one head.
6. A pastor must have
7. A good testimony.
   - A godly personal character.
   - An ability to minister effectively.
   - A model Christian family.

If you lose your testimony, you lose your ministry. Keep a good name!

GPS (GETTING THE PRINCIPLES SUMMARIZED)

Find answers to these questions in the chapter.

Biblical Words for the Pastor
1. How many offices now exist in the local church?
2. What New Testament words mean the same thing as pastor?

The Continuing Ministry of Evangelists and Pastors
3. What is the difference between the evangelist and the pastor?
4. Who chooses a pastor?

The Qualifications of a Pastor
5. The book lists four scriptural qualifications for a pastor. Paraphrase each and give a verse, or part of a verse, for each.

APPles (Applying the Principles Practically)

Apply these ideas to your church. Discussion will often go beyond just the facts in the reading.

Biblical Words for the Pastor
1. Should a church have bishops and elders as well as pastors and deacons? Defend your answer from Scripture.

The Foundation of the Apostles and Prophets
2. Based on Ephesians 2:20, why are there no apostles and prophets today?

The Qualifications of a Pastor: A Model Christian Family
3. Can a man be a pastor if he has never been married? If he is divorced? Divorced and remarried?
4. What is the difference between a "model Christian family" and a "perfect Christian family"?

THE WORK OF A PASTOR

Take heed therefore unto yourselves, and to all the flock, over the which the Holy Ghost hath made you overseers, to feed the church of God, which he hath purchased with his own blood.
Acts 20:28

Some people jokingly say, "It must be nice to be a pastor and only work one or two days a week!" Anyone who has spent much time around a pastor, however, knows that such a statement does not represent pastoral work. Ephesians 4:12 says that God gave pastor-teachers to local churches "for the perfecting of the saints"—the members of the local church—so that they are effective in "the work of the ministry, for the edifying of the body of Christ." The *ultimate* goal of a pastor's never-ending labors is nothing less than Christlikeness in his people and in himself. Romans 8:29 promises, "For whom he did foreknow, he also did predestinate to be conformed to the image of his Son, that he might be the firstborn among many brethren." Every pastor labors to take part in this process of conformity to Christ, a process that is never complete in this life. What a task!

In order to function properly in his pastoral work, a pastor must have his priorities in order: "The steps of a good man are ordered by the Lord: and he delighteth in his way" (Psalm 37:23). There are two areas of priority that a pastor must consider—his personal priorities and his ministry priorities. Both are important and must be carefully handled if a pastor wants to be successful in his personal and professional life.

Paul addressed the pastor's awesome task in his farewell to the Ephesian elders, which Luke recorded in Acts 20:17-38. Whatever Paul felt burdened to say to these pastors in this last personal encounter would be highly significant. It is no coincidence that, in giving pastors something like a job description, three main responsibilities are prominent: "Take heed therefore *unto yourselves*, and *to all the flock*, over the which the Holy Ghost hath made you overseers, *to feed the church of God*, which he hath purchased with his own blood" (verse 28). The pastor has the personal priority of his own walk with the Lord, including his care of his family; and he has the ministry priorities of overseeing the church and of feeding the flock.

A TRUE-LIFE EXAMPLE: THE LONG-HAIRED, HIPPY TYPE

Not only did Ron look out of place, with his long hair halfway down his back, he must have felt out of place too. When I was the associate pastor of another work, Ron showed up in my college and career age Sunday school class one morning. He had a testimony of being recently saved and seemed sincere enough, but that first Sunday, he challenged me with "Why do you people make such a big deal out of hair?" The work of the pastor is all about people, but how do you help someone like this?

THE RESPONSIBILITY OF A PERSONAL WALK

The Pastor's Relationship to God

Paul gave priority to the personal walk of the church leaders themselves. The first instruction to the Ephesian elders was, "Take heed therefore unto yourselves." One's own walk with the Lord is, of course, the most important element of any Christian's private life, and a pastor is no exception. For the pastor, however, his personal walk is also incalculably important to the effectiveness of his ministry. A pastor simply cannot expect from his people what he does not seek to model in his own life. If he wants the people in his church to be holy, he must seek to be holy. If he wants the people in his church to pray, he must pray. If he wants the people in his church to witness, he must personally proclaim the Gospel too. If he expects the men in his church to be godly husbands and fathers, he must do much more than teach on the subject: he must show the way by being a godly husband and father himself. If he wants the people to love him, he must love them and show them how to love each other. To put it briefly, the best thing a pastor can do for his church is to live a consistent Christian life himself.

Your walk talks,
And your talk talks;
But your walk talks louder than your talk talks.

A pastor cannot expect from his people what he does not seek to model in his own life.

This publicly visible consistency will only come from a consistent and sincere time between the pastor and God alone. In Acts 6, the deacons were selected in the early church to allow pastors to have more time for preaching and prayer (Acts 6:5). The pastor who wants to effectively do the work of the ministry must make sure he gives proper attention to these two areas. He must have a regular, consistent prayer life that remembers the people, problems, and programs of the local church. He should have a record of many prayers answered in the past and should be praying, in faith believing, for ministry victories in the future. The pastor must be consistent in personal evangelism: witnessing to and winning people to Christ one-on-one, not just in his preaching. He should have a regularly scheduled study time throughout each week so that he will be properly prepared for the messages he preaches. He should also be a constant reader of ministry-related books and magazines so that he can keep his mind sharp and his understanding of issues current. He should be consistently aware of current events, both in the Christian and secular society. It is obvious in the Scriptures that God wants the pastor to give himself to the study of the Bible and to praying for God's people.

The Pastor's Home

One of the pastor's greatest personal priorities is summed up in the phrase "family first." For years there has been a debate about the balance between family responsibilities and ministry responsibilities. Which is most important? The answer seems very clear to me when we read the qualifications of a pastor listed in I Timothy 3. In verses 4 and 5 the Bible says a pastor must be "one that ruleth well his own house, having his children in subjection with all gravity; (For if a man know not how to rule his own house, how shall he take care of the church of God?)" It is clear that a man does not qualify to be a pastor unless he has his home and family under control. Therefore, among a pastor's personal responsibilitites "family first" must be his motto.

The most important relationship in the home for the pastor is his marriage relationship. The Bible says he should be "the husband of one wife" (I Timothy 3:2). This means that he has never been divorced and has a committed relationship to one woman until death. It is important to raise godly children in a pastor's home; however, this will not be accomplished well if the pastor and his wife do not have a wonderful Christ-honoring relationship. Too many pastors burn out in the ministry and lose their families. The best thing a husband and wife can give their children is the security and example of a good marriage. A pastor must love his wife as Christ loved the church and gave Himself for it (Ephesians 5:25). He should live a consistent testimony at home and in the community. His wife and children should see him as a steady, Christlike example. If a pastor keeps "family first," he will have the joy not only of seeing his children serving the Lord but also of seeing his children raise his grandchildren for the Lord.

To say "family first" is not giving pastors an excuse to be lazy in the ministry. The average layman in our churches is expected to work a 40-50 hour week at a secular job and still volunteer time for the local church ministry. Therefore, I believe the average pastor should give at least 50-60 hours to the ministry of the local church weekly. (This takes into account even the time spent in regular church services as part of that cumulative time.) I learned, however, that many of my responsibilities could be done with my family. I do not neglect my family for the ministry, but neither do I neglect the ministry for my family. A pastor's wife and children need to see a dedicated, hard-working leader in their home and church. This example will set the pace not only for church leadership but also for family members as well. Proverbs tells us, "Go to the ant, thou sluggard, consider her ways and be wise" (Proverbs 6:6). This is a good section of Scripture for the pastor since he must work diligently for the good of his family, his church, and, ultimately, the cause of Christ.

One practical way to keep right priorities is to establish a weekly schedule. Sunday is very busy for the pastor. However, at the same time, the family is involved in the local church as well. Monday night is family night in our household. Every family needs at least one night each week dedicated to family time, enjoying each other's company and communication. Tuesday night is devoted to visitation and sometimes to school activities. When my children were in school, we did many of the school activities together. It is also good to take your children on visitation with you. My wife and I also enjoy visiting people together. Wednesday night is our mid-week service. In our church it is considered the family service. Young people provide all the special music; families sit together (on Sunday night, we have a youth meeting and a children's ministry at the same time as the auditorium service); and messages are designed to be practical and, many times, applicable to the home. Thursday night is again left as a family time for our church families. The pastor may need to do more visitation or may have some counseling sessions on that night. If so, he should plan to take some time off during the day to spend with his wife and children. Friday night is always busy with church or school activities. Most of these activities, again, are attended by all family members. Saturday is a good day to set aside to do projects around the home and for get-aways with the family. I always try to go to bed early on Saturday night so that I will be refreshed and ready for the busy Sunday.

Something else that can be done with family members is to have lunch together on a regular basis. The joy of a pastor's schedule is its flexibility. He should take some time with his wife for little outings, and he should have personal time with each of his children. My wife really enjoys having breakfast together away from the home. Sometimes I even set up appointments with my sons at my office so I can have personal communication with them. To prioritize properly, a schedule is essential.

Another important aspect of a pastor's making "family first" is a family vacation. This should be scheduled at least once a year, and it should be designed to have fun with the family. Too many pastors have made vacations ministry trips rather than recreational trips. There may be some cross-over on Sundays, but the rest of the week should be for fun and relaxation with the family. The pastor's family needs to have fun with their father as well as ministering with him.

It is wise for a pastor and his wife to get away from the local church—and even the local area—at least once a quarter. I suggest renting a hotel room someplace a short drive away, where the pastor and his wife can simply relax, communicate, and plan future activities. A pastor and his wife should be praying together regularly, but, these getaway times can provide extra time for concentrated prayer about specific problems and projects. My wife and I have found that just the drive to the getaway can be a wonderful, relaxing time of quality communication. The pastor's schedule is very busy and many times even his home is not a haven. Therefore, a little getaway from time to time can give the refreshment necessary to refocus the pastor and his wife on the ministry to which God has called them.

The Pastor as Servant Leader

The subject of servant leadership deserves further examination here. When I think of servant leadership, I think of Ken Collier, the director of The WILDS Christian Camp. Arriving one Saturday before I was to speak at a couple's retreat, I needed to talk over some matters with him. He was not in his office. It was a beautiful day, but, no, he was not walking on the grounds. I found him in the main meeting room of the lodge—with a mop and bucket. All the staff had clean-up jobs to do, getting ready for the upcoming week, before they had their Saturday time off, even Ken. He took the responsibility of cleaning the lodge meeting room and the restroom adjacent to it.

Not long ago, Ken brought on a new staff member who would be overseeing another branch of the WILDS ministry. The new staff member, who had a wife and five children, would work with him at the North Carolina camp, learning the details and absorbing the philosophy of the ministry. The only available housing on the campsite was a small cottage. Since the Colliers' children were grown and all married except for one, who was off to college most of the year, the Colliers moved into the cottage and insisted that the new staff member take their house for the duration of their stay. This kind of servant leadership is a virtue which, perhaps more than any other, is impossible to teach apart from consistent modeling.

A pastor is completely unable to cultivate a servant spirit among his people if he does not make service his own habit of life. Like the Chief Shepherd Himself, every under-shepherd should be seeking ways to minister, rather than opportunities to be ministered to (Matthew 20:28). Far too often, a pastor tries to persuade people to give of their time, talents, and treasures when he himself is not willing to make such sacrifices.

So how does a pastor maintain a personal walk with the Lord? Where does he find the power to be a model for his people? The key to spiritual growth is the same for pastors and laymen alike: "Walk in the Spirit and ye shall not fulfill the lust of the flesh" (Galatians 5:16). He must be daily filled with the Spirit and living according to the Scriptures.

THE RESPONSIBILITY FOR THE MINSITRY

The Responsibility of Oversight

The first of the ministry responsibilities spelled out in Paul's exhortation is that of *oversight*. He commanded the elders, "Take heed . . . to all the flock over the which the Holy Ghost hath made you overseers." This means the pastor has an administrative role. He must use his authority and organizational skills to make sure the Lord's work is being accomplished in and through the lives of people whom the Holy Spirit has entrusted to his care. The deacons and other members of the church cannot be mindful on a daily basis of what is going on in the church, but the pastor must be.

The pastor may delegate but the ultimate responsibility rests on his shoulders.

Hebrews 13:17 says, "Obey them that have the rule over you, and submit yourselves: for they watch for your souls, as they that must give account, that they may do it with joy, and not with grief." This is a command to laymen, but let us consider the implication it has for the pastor. Because he will answer for the spiritual well-being of his people, the pastor must exercise authority to make sure that needs are being met. Failure to properly "watch for" the souls of his congregation means that the pastor will face "grief" when he gives account of his life's work. If the word grief seems like an understatement, it may be because there are no words adequate to express the depth of shame and loss of such a moment. Likewise, the word "joy" must be only a small indication of the sense of standing before the Lord and hearing His "well done."

The pastor teaches his people to minister to each other and to lost souls. As an administrator of programs and projects, a great part of the pastor's day-to-day concern is the constant improvement of the effectiveness of the church's evangelism and discipleship ministries. The pastor should multiply his efforts by bringing in others to help: deacons, volunteers, and, if the ministry size and budget warrant, other staff. Even though the pastor may delegate authority to others, he can never afford to forget that the ultimate responsibility rests on his shoulders. He would do well to heed some ancient advice: "Be thou diligent to know the state of thy flocks, and look well to thy herds" (Proverbs 27:23).

The Priorities of Ministry

In operating a local church, it is important for the pastor to understand his ministry goals and priorities. Decisions need to be made with these priorities in mind. Finances need to be budgeted with these priorities in mind. Time should be allotted with these priorities in mind. A pastor must prioritize his life and the ministry if he wants to have maximum efficiency.

1. Philosophy

The first priority in the ministry is to have the right philosophy. A person's philosophy is the system of values and beliefs that guides his actions. It involves the pastor's beliefs about the operation of the local church ministry. The Bible is our guide for every area of life and ministry. Therefore, the pastor must formulate a biblical philosophy of ministry. He should never compromise the goal of producing Christlike character in the lives of believers (Romans 8:29; Philippians 2:5; Ephesians 4:13). Everything that is done in the local ministry should help develop Christlikeness.

Colossians 2:8 provides an important reminder: "Beware lest any man spoil you through philosophy and vain deceit, after the tradition of men, after the rudiments of the world, and not after Christ." The pastor must watch for the false philosophies of the world that are creeping into local church ministries. The popular errors, with variations and camouflage, are many:

- Big is good in itself.
- Give people what they want.
- Music is amoral.
- Ecumenism.

- Humanism.
- Pragmatism.
- Materialism.

Philosophy is the pastor's number one priority. That is why we are exhorted to "earnestly contend for the faith which was once delivered unto the saints" (Jude 3). The right philosophy is essential to achieving the right success.

2. People

The second priority for the pastor and his ministry is people. The pastor's job is to perfect the saints for the work of the ministry (Ephesians 4:12). In order to do so, he must preach the Word of God and promote its biblical philosophy (II Timothy 4:2). People should be the priority in a local church, not finances, buildings, or special programs. Jesus Christ came, lived, and died for people. Pastors are under-shepherds for the Savior. Therefore, we should live our lives for people as well.

People are also the essential ingredient in producing a quality ministry. Only as we perfect the saints to do the work of the ministry will the body be edified. The pastor cannot do all the work but should commit the work to faithful men who can teach others also (II Timothy 2:2). Finding good people to take responsibility for the work in the local church is a very important priority for the pastor. The better the people, the better the work. The wiser the selection, the more positive the progress. People are the key to having a ministry, expanding a ministry, and reproducing a ministry. Reaching people, discipling people, selecting people, training people, and motivating people should be priorities for every pastor.

One of the more unlikely looking people early in my ministry was Ron. Recently saved, he still had much of the old lifestyle clinging to him, including hair hanging halfway down his back. The first Sunday he came to the college and career class I taught, he was waiting for me after class.

"Why do you people make such a big deal out of hair?" he asked.

I had to suppress a smile. I hadn't said anything about hair in that class, but I had asked that same question a few years before when I was a worldly businessman, wearing hair over my ears in the style of the time. I gave him the same answer a wise pastor gave me: "We aren't making a big deal out of it, you are. You are welcome, and accepted, and loved, just as you are. It's just that any organization has standards for leadership, even secular ones like IBM. To be in a leadership position here, like teaching, we require a little higher standard. Certain hair or dress styles are associated, for some, with certain lifestyles, and we do not want to send a mixed message to those we lead."

He accepted that. But hair was not the only question he had. Every Sunday he would be waiting with questions after the morning service. They were deep questions, revealing a probing mind and a real desire to know God. It was not only his knowledge that was growing. He was growing spiritually, putting away the sins of the old life, becoming that "new creature" in Christ.

I had him over to my home often. I genuinely loved him, accepted him, and wanted to see him grow in the Lord. In a few years he was off to a Christian college and then to seminary. Now he is a professor at Heartland Theological Seminary, a ministry of the church I pastor.

3. Programs

The third priority in ministry is to have the right programs. These programs must be consistent with the church's philosophy. They also must be a right fit for the people in the local ministry and be beneficial to the people of that ministry. Buying someone else's pre-packaged program, however effective the program has been elsewhere, is not always the way to go. You do not have to reinvent the wheel, but you do need to let your people adapt an idea to fit the gifts and callings that they have. There should be programs for evangelism of the lost, edification of the saved, and exaltation of the Savior. There should be programs for children, teenagers, and adults. There should be programs in the church, and outside the church in the community. Programs should be staffed by the people in the church who have the right biblical philosophy. They should be adapted to meet the time and culture of the community in which one ministers, but they should never compromise the biblical philosophy of the ministry. Having programs must never take priority over having qualified people in the ministry. Programs are important, but not most important.

4. Properties

Properties are the last priority in the ministry. Sad to say, many times in our society it seems that churches have made buildings their number one goal. Many dollars have been wasted on large, expensive buildings, money that could have been invested much more effectively in people and programs, both in our country and around the world. It is nice to have a quality auditorium in which to meet; however, extravagant buildings may waste precious dollars that could be better used in reaching the community and the world for Jesus Christ. No ministry should limit their personnel or programs because of large mortgages on properties. Buildings should be adequate and attractive, but not extravagant and expensive.

One thing I have learned about properties is the importance of getting sufficient land. If in doubt, it is better to err on the side of getting too much land rather than not enough land. Many ministries have become land locked because of their short-sightedness. It is much easier to sell off additional property you do not need in future years than it is to purchase property you need then. Therefore, I encourage churches to purchase as much property as possible when locating a church ministry rather than getting by with the minimum. Sometimes land can be purchased with a contracted option to purchase more at a fixed price. That would accomplish the same goal without the immediate outlay of finances. Ministry can be accomplished through people without properties. However, properties have never accomplished ministry by themselves. That is why they should be the fourth priority in a pastor's mind, not the first.

Second Timothy 2:2 gives the top three priorities in one verse: "The things that though has heard of me among many witnesses"—philosophy—"the same commit thou to faithful men"—people—"who shall be able to teach others also"—programs. Properties are not mentioned, even though necessary, unless the hardship mentioned in verse 3 is talking about our buildings (and many times this may be the case). If the pastor keeps his ministry priorities right, God can bless his efforts and the work of the local church.

The Responsibility of Feeding the Flock

The other ministry responsibility in Acts 20:28 is that of *feeding the flock*. This refers to preaching and teaching God's Word to God's people so that they profit spiritually. Passionate, biblical preaching may not be the latest ministerial fad in contemporary Christianity, but it occupies a place of honor in the New Testament. God has chosen preaching—the *foolishness* of preaching, in the eyes of natural men—to wage war against the counterfeit wisdom of this world (I Corinthians 1:18-27). If the Word of God is profitable for doctrine, reproof, correction, and instruction in righteousness—and it is (II Timothy 3:16)—then the shepherd of the flock must be "instant in season, out of season," always ready to "reprove, rebuke, exhort with all longsuffering and doctrine" (II Timothy 4:2). The preaching of the Word is intended to motivate people to action. By earnest, bold, presentation of the Word, the pastor shows his people what God says and urges them to take action. A pastor who is not a preacher of the Word is a shepherd with lazy, complacent sheep!

A well-fed flock enjoys good teaching, which complements the preaching.

In addition to being a preacher, a pastor must be an able teacher. He is, in fact, called a *pastor-teacher* in Ephesians 4:11. A well-fed flock enjoys good teaching, which complements—it completes, or rounds out—the preaching. While preaching should be motivational, teaching ought to be educational. While preaching challenges people to obey the Word of God, stressing the "why" of obedience, teaching explains the biblical principles, that is, the "what" and "how" of obedience.

A particularly challenging but exciting facet of feeding the flock is teaching people to feed themselves. Babies must be fed, but adults feed themselves, and the achievement of spiritual maturity among church members is a high priority. A pastor must instruct new believers, not only in basic doctrines, but also in developing both the ability to study and the habit of studying, the Word of God for themselves. A pastor will know he is enjoying some success when his people feed themselves and are, as a result, "no more children, tossed to and fro, and carried about with every wind of doctrine, by the sleight of men, and cunning craftiness, whereby they lie in wait to deceive" (Ephesians 4:14). A pastor who is not a teacher of the Word is a shepherd with starving sheep!

The pastor is responsible for making sure the flock is properly fed, but that is not to say that he does all the preaching and teaching himself. A wise pastor will utilize the ministry of an evangelist, whether for a week of special meetings or for particular Sunday services. God gave evangelists to local churches to complement the ministry of pastors. In bringing souls to Christ, as well as in educating and energizing believers, evangelists greatly enrich the spiritual life of a congregation. If a church is blessed with an evangelist within its membership, the pastor and evangelist can maximize their complementary ministries, working hand in hand for the perfecting of the saints.

God has also gifted other believers in the area of teaching (Romans 12:7). As a pastor begins to recognize people who can teach, he should put them to work! What church could succeed without godly Sunday school teachers? And what church could not benefit from the expertise of laymen in such areas as finance, marriage, and child-rearing? Of course, a church with a Christian school would not last a day without several teachers specializing in various ages and academic subjects. Praise God for laymen who have the gift of teaching!

Much more could be said about the work of the pastor in the local church. Many good books have been written on that topic. One last, balanced perspective is extremely important: the pastor must do his work in the power of the Holy Spirit (Ephesians 5:18) and always in an attitude of prayer (I Thessalonians 5:17). We must remember the truth taught by our Lord Jesus Christ, "For without me ye can do nothing" (John 15:5). At the same time we should remember the confidence of the Apostle Paul, "I can do all things through Christ which strengtheneth me" (Philippians 4:13). May God help all pastors to do His work through His strength, for His glory.

To say the least, a pastor bears a heavy load of responsibilities—a personal walk with the Lord, oversight of the ministry, and the feeding the flock. But as the pastor and the people alike walk in the Spirit and take up their responsibilities, the church will be built up, and the work of Jesus Christ will be expanded. How long does this work go on? "Till we all come in the unity of the faith, and of the knowledge of the Son of God, unto a perfect man, unto the measure of the stature of the fulness of Christ" (Ephesians 4:13). To put it another way, we will *never* run out of work to do until Jesus comes again; it is only when "he shall appear" that "we shall be like him" (I John 3:2).

This, furthermore, means that pastors should be training young pastors to carry on the work in their place if the Lord tarries. The personalities may change, but the office stays the same, and the responsibilities outlined in Acts 20:28 must be carried out until Jesus comes again.

CHAPTER REVIEW

1. The pastor's ultimate goal is to lead his people into Christlikeness.
2. The pastor's first responsibility is to be what he wants his people to be.
   - He must maintain his personal walk with God.
   - He must maintain his relationship with his family.
   - He must demonstrate servant leadership.
3. The organization and administration of the church is the pastor's special, daily responsibility.
4. The pastor must make decisions on the basis of priorities:
   - First, philosophy.
   - Second, people.
   - Third, program.
   - Fourth, properties.
5. The goal of this organization and administration is to improve the effectiveness of the church's evangelism and discipleship.
6. Preach the Word: motivate!
7. Teach the Word: provide practical instruction!
8. Enlist the aid of church members who are gifted as teachers.
9. The pastor's work will only be finished when Christ returns and His people are transformed to His likeness in His presence.
10. The pastor should be training those who will come after him.

The responsibility is awesome: Walk in the Spirit!

 GPS (GETTING THE PRINCIPLES SUMMARIZED)

Find answers to these questions in the chapter.

Introduction

1. What are the areas that Paul exhorts the Ephesian elders to take heed to? (Acts 20:28)

2. The purpose of all Christians is to glorify God (Isaiah 43:7), but what is the specific goal of pastoral ministry?

The Pastor's Relationship to God
3. What is the best thing a pastor can do for his church?

The Pastor's Home
4. What is the best thing a husband and wife can give their children?
5. What are the author's terms for the two broad areas of a pastor's responsibilities?

The Pastor's Relationship to God
6. What is the most important priority of a pastor?
7. What is the source of "publicly visible consistency"?

The Pastor's Home
8. How can the pastor maintain a personal life for himself and his family? Note: the same things are equally helpful for a deacon – or any Christian husband – and his family.
9. How much time, on average, should a pastor schedule for ministry work each week? What does the text give as a reason for that amount of time?

The Pastor as Servant-Leader
10. How does a pastor develop a servant-spirit in his people?

The Responsibility of Oversight
11. What are the two broad areas of the pastor's responsibility for ministry? (Acts 20:28)
12. What does Hebrews 13:17 imply for the pastor?

The Priorities of Ministry
13. What are the four priorities of ministry?

The Responsibility to Feed the Flock
14. What is the purpose of preaching?
15. In addition to the pastor, who else teaches in the church?

APPles (Applying the Principles Practically)

Apply these ideas to your church. Discussion will often go beyond just the facts in the reading.

Introduction
1. What does it mean to "take heed to" something? (Acts 20:28)

The Pastor's Relationship to God
2. What specific things does the book mention as important for a pastor in order to be effective in ministry?
3. Which of these areas do you feel is your next area for personal growth? Why is it important – that is, what can happen to promote the Kingdom of God if you work on that? What specific steps can you take?

The Priorities of Ministry
4. Make the case that the four priorities have an order of importance.

THE OFFICE AND QUALIFICATIONS OF A DEACON

Likewise must the deacons be grave, not doubletongued, not given to much wine, not greedy of filthy lucre.
I Timothy 3:8

I hope that the deacons at your church are the kind of blessing that God designed them to be. You have probably heard of situations where people entrusted with the office of deacon have grieved the heart of God, broken the trust of the congregation, and have caused the enemies of God to mock His church. Perhaps you have even endured such a situation. The biblical role of the deacon has been the subject of a long and continuing discussion. We should look, not at what history or denominations have said, but rather at what the Bible says about the function, qualifications, and selection of deacons in the local, New Testament church.

A TRUE-LIFE EXAMPLE: THE NEW AGE COMES TO WORK

The management seminar was not too unusual: nice hotel, brightly lit meeting room, speaker's rostrum up front. Every year the company would send managers to something like this to reinforce old skills and learn new ones. But this time the new "workplace skill" was going to be harder to swallow than the free bagels in the hotel lobby. What do you do when you find New Age philosophy and practice, very contrary to the Christian stand you have been taking, being pushed onto the workforce?

THE OFFICE OF DEACONS

The Nature of the Office

God gave the local church two offices, the pastor and the deacon. Deacons are not so much men who are ordained for the purpose of ministering the Word of God as they are laymen who are selected for furthering the total work of the ministry. To see the fullness of what God designed, in contrast to what people have sometimes developed, let us consider what deacons are and are not.

Deacons Are Not

Consider three things that deacons are not. First, they are not pastors. They are not overseers appointed by God to direct, to lead, and to establish the vision for the local church. Second, they are not merely a committee. A committee is usually a group appointed by the church for the purpose of carrying out a specific duty. Deacons have a plurality of duties determined by the needs of the church. Those particular duties are not highly defined in the Scriptures. Third, deacons are not a board. A board has executive power; it has the right and power to rule. The New Testament saints never seemed to have anyone over them except the chosen man of God. Furthermore, the work of deacons is a spiritual ministry, not necessarily a work of corporate business or finances. Some states require that there be "trustees" with legal authority to sign documents. It is also a great help—as well as a safeguard—for the pastor to have others working with him on financial matters. These tasks may be specific committee functions for some of the deacons as their way to serve. The key thing is to maintain the attitude of a servant, not of an overlord, whatever your specific duties are.

Deacons Are

The biblical view, then, is that deacons are the selected servants of the church to do whatever work must be done within the church to meet the needs of the people and to free up the pastor for prayer and for the ministry of the Word.

Deacons are appointed servants. They are men appointed to their tasks, as described in Acts 6. Because the church had grown so fast, there were great needs. The church had baptized thousands of people in the first six months. On the day of Pentecost alone, there were three thousand saved, and, maybe just days later, Acts 4:4 states that the "number of the men was about five thousand." People were being added to the church every day. I think the church was growing so fast they were not able to determine exactly how many people were part of it. One unexpected result of this rapid growth was that some people began to murmur and complain to the apostles that some widows were being helped and others were not. Deacons did not exist in the early church until there was a need for them—a problem—and then they were selected by the "congregation" and appointed by the apostles to alleviate the burden on the men who were praying and studying the Word of God for the public ministry. In this way they helped in the fulfillment of the apostles' God-given work. After the deacons had been selected and approved by the people, and after the apostles had laid hands on them, it seems that the apostles began to appoint them to their work. The immediate need was to take care of the tables of the widows.

The same standards apply to deacons as to preachers.

Deacons are to be examples of Christian faith. They are to have the same qualifications, the same stringent rules, as the bishop or elder. There are to be no more inconsistencies in their lives than in the lives of the men who are actually ministering the Word of God. Paul tells us in I Timothy 3 that the same standards apply to deacons as to preachers: "A bishop then must be blameless. . . . *Likewise* must the deacons be grave" (verses 2 and 8, emphasis added).

Deacons may sometimes be preachers. Deacon Stephen brought a tremendous message defending the faith for which he later died. His sermon had all the ingredients of the Gospel—the death, burial, and resurrection of Jesus Christ. In Acts 21 Deacon Philip was called "Philip the evangelist, which was one of the seven." Acts 8 tells that he preached Christ in the city of Samaria, was directed by God to give the Ethiopian eunuch the Gospel of Christ, and then was miraculously transported to Azotus. He apparently was left to ground transport then, "and passing through he preached in all the cities, till he came to Caesarea" (v. 40).

Origin as a Key to Purpose

Deacons originated for a definite purpose. Deacons did not originate as denominational liaisons. I know some churches where the deacons have greater rapport with the denominational director than they do with the pastor and may circumvent the pastor, going directly to denominational headquarters to get what they want. Consequently, if the pastor happens to be leading them as God directs, but the deacons disagree, they may go to the denominational liaison and join forces to remove that pastor from his God-given position.

Second, these men were not in charge of the church. I think I have arrived at a partial understanding of how that idea originated. Many pastors in the South in years gone by would pastor three or four churches. They did not really pastor the churches; they were the preachers. They would visit the churches and preach the gospel at various intervals. The deacons were the people who lived in the community and cared for the building, the grounds, and the spiritual welfare of the church. If the preacher did not like a particular action by the deacons, he could just resign, of course, and that church would then have to find somebody else to fill the position of preacher. The preacher who resigned would then concentrate on the other three or four churches where he preached. Soon small churches began joining together for other purposes, such as supporting missionaries, running youth camps, operating Bible colleges, and publishing literature. Eventually, they became denominational bodies. As a result of that, these deacons felt that, if their church was to have any continuity in its personality, its program, and its purpose—that is, if it were to continue as a local, New Testament church—they would have to take the leadership. After all, the preacher may be gone tomorrow. However, once God gives a full-time pastor, it is no longer the responsibility of the deacons to be in charge of the church.

Third, they are not the financial wizards and business managers of the church. I certainly think that a wise pastor and a wise people will seek the counsel of these men, but that is not their primary purpose. It is an erroneous idea on the part of the average deacon that his purpose is to control the moneybags and to see to it that the church is operating with proper financial guidelines. The operational standard for a local church is different from that of an ordinary business. The church is a living organism based upon the Word of God and the headship of Jesus Christ. He will not let His church fail if its affairs are conducted according to His commandments and according to His leadership in unique situations, even though that leadership sometimes may seem to defy traditional business practices. In chapter nine we will discuss the matter of church finances in more detail.

Acts 6 presents a remarkably different purpose in the origin of the office. Deacons originated at a time of murmuring and trouble. The first deacons served as peacemakers. "And in those days, when the number of the disciples was multiplied, there arose a murmuring of the Grecians against the Hebrews . . ." and the deacons were drafted not only to meet the needs of the widows but also to dispel the murmuring. Some pastors talk about having difficulty with their deacons. Sometimes deacons and pastors seem to be enemies within the church. This relationship is not what God intended. Truthfully, the greatest work that deacons may do is that of serving as peacemakers. Once, a leader of a good Christian organization in another state had a difference of opinion with my pastor. It was a matter on which good, fundamental, Bible-believing people disagree. The subject of the disagreement is not so important as the way in which this other man was handling it. He wrote letters attacking our pastor on this point and sent them to the people in his state. I called him to discuss the matter. First, I listened . . . and listened . . . and listened. The emotionally charged tone of his voice and his accusations ranging beyond a simple point of Bible interpretation gave me an understanding that this was not just a matter of seeking theological purity. This man had an attitude of personal animosity. When he was finished, I said, "He's my pastor; I know him; and I see none of these things you are talking about. When you attack our pastor, you are attacking our church. You can hold your opinions, but you need to leave us alone." I regret that this other leader never sought reconciliation with my pastor, but at least the attacks stopped. Sometimes when we plead our own cause, we are suspected of just wanting to defend ourselves; but, when someone else takes up our defense, that defense has greater credibility, even though the same information is presented. The deacon can effectively defuse unjust criticisms directed against the pastor.

On another occasion, a staff member insisted that the church change insurance carriers. As a deacon helping with this area, I could not see the benefit of the change. As I talked with him, I brought up a phrase common in the IBM philosophy: "If it's not broke, don't fix it." I asked, "Is it broken? How is this change going to make things better?" When this staff member was not able to express to me any clear gain to be made in the change, he was willing to let the matter drop.

Sometimes the deacon can make peace by helping people sort through their own ideas and see the practical (in this case) or biblical viewpoint on a topic.

But I need to offer three cautions here.

- First, avoid the extreme of defending your pastor "right or wrong." Realize that sometimes the best help you can be to your pastor is to help him see things he may be unaware of regarding himself or his ministry. There is a right way and a wrong way to do this (I Timothy 5:19). This matter is discussed more in chapter ten, "Dealing with Difficulties."
- Second, avoid taking up an offense against someone who is angry against your pastor or your church. One characteristic of a godly person is that he does not take up a reproach against another (Psalm 15:3), but in meekness he instructs those who are self-defeating in their unreasoning opposition (II Timothy 2:25).
- Third, be a problem solver, not merely a gossip receiver. I am reminded of a conversation that our associate pastor had with a certain church member. The church member said, "I don't know why everyone comes to me with their complaints." The associate pastor replied, "I do. They know you'll listen to them." If you make people get together with the person against whom they have a complaint and resolve their problems biblically, people will stop coming to you with gossip!

Not only were the first deacons peacemakers, but they were also extra helpers. The deacons assisted in the work overload of the pastors. The pastors had become so involved in ministering the Word of God that they could not take care of all the widows, the orphans, the hurting saints, or hospital visitations, to use present-day vernacular. The deacons were placed in charge of the time-consuming work of "the daily ministration" to allow the men of God the necessary time to minister the Word of God, to win souls, and to spend time in prayer. The deacons received assignments and were appointed by these pastors to do particular tasks which developed into a great ministry.

The duties of deacons are not described exactly in the Scripture, and for good reason. Perhaps some deacons would see a short list of tasks and think that was all they had to do! The particular assignment of Acts 6, to "serve tables," is representative of the broad picture of freeing up pastors. As the apostles requested men to meet the immediate need, it is left up to the church leaders—now the pastors—to direct the deacons in what needs to be done. Therein lies the assignment of the deacon.

In the beginning, then, the deacons were selected to meet needs—to serve—so that the church leaders, the Apostles, could concentrate on the ministry of the Word and prayer. A need was identified, and "the twelve called the multitude of disciples unto them" and told them to "look ye out among you seven men of honest report, full of the Holy Ghost and wisdom, whom we may appoint over this business." These seven were then brought to the apostles; the apostles laid hands on them; "and the word of God increased; and the number of the disciples multiplied in Jerusalem greatly; and a great company of the priests were obedient to the faith." May your church so flourish because of your service!

THE QUALIFICATIONS OF DEACONS

The guidelines for the selection of deacons are the highest mentioned in the Scriptures; they equal the standards for elders and the bishops, or pastors.

Two Key Passages

1. From Acts
Then the twelve called the multitude of disciples unto them, and said, It is not reason that we should leave the word of God, and serve tables. Wherefore, brethren, look ye out among you seven men of honest report, full of the Holy Ghost and wisdom, whom we may appoint over this business. And the saying pleased the whole multitude: and they chose Stephen, a man full of faith and of the Holy Ghost.
Acts 6:2-5

A deacon must be a man "of honest report." First, you must do right, not only within the church, but also in your community. The deacon's reputation becomes the reputation of the church. Therefore, being fallible as we are, you must be ready to make things right when you fall short. Be willing to take responsibility for your own actions so that God does not get the blame.

A deacon must be "full of the Holy Ghost and of wisdom." We all live very busy lives, but we must be careful to maintain our personal relationship with God. Many years ago, a great pastor made this observation: "On Sunday morning, the average church could carry on ninety percent of its operation just as effectively if the Holy Spirit had departed from it." Is our work in the church so mechanical that we would not miss the Holy Spirit? Is our work dependent only on human organization without real dependence on divine anointing so that we would not miss the Holy Spirit if He were not in our music, if He were not in our preaching, if He were not in our Sunday school? Have we become so insensitive that we could permit the divine presence of the Holy Spirit to be absent and not even miss Him? I fear that, if we would be doggedly honest, we would have to admit that we do much of what we do without His presence. He is the cutting edge on the ax. He is that blessed Holy Spirit that makes a failure successful and makes the mediocre great. The greatest duties you have toward your preacher and your church are to pray for them and to be a Spirit-filled man.

Deacons are to be "full of faith." The Bible says, "Whatsoever is not of faith is sin" (Romans 14:23) and "Without faith it is impossible to please him" (Hebrews 11:6). Now, faith is not foolishness. There is a difference between reckless faith and reckless foolishness. Faith is that which believes that God will do what He said He would do, and we can act on His promises. There are many things that have no Scriptural basis; therefore, they are not of faith but of the flesh.

Acts chapter 7 gives us another view of the deacon. He must be able to witness, to teach, and to preach if necessary. Stephen preached a powerful message before the Sanhedrin. We also see Deacon Philip preaching and teaching in Acts 8. No deacon, pastor, or leader who is not a witness will be effective very long. A deacon should have a sermon in the back of his mind and should be ready to preach it.

Another requirement is a willingness to die for the faith, as seen at the end of Acts 7. We may be living in times when many Christians will have to suffer for the faith in our "civilized" western countries, even as many have suffered in the past and are suffering around the world right now. I personally believe our current peace is only the lull before the storm. Are you willing to die for the faith?

2. From I Timothy

This is a true saying, If a man desire the office of a bishop, he desireth a good work. A bishop then must be blameless, the husband of one wife, vigilant, sober, of good behaviour, given to hospitality, apt to teach; Not given to wine, no striker, not greedy of filthy lucre; but patient, not a brawler, not covetous; One that ruleth well his own house, having his children in subjection with all gravity; (For if a man know not how to rule his own house, how shall he take care of the church of God?) Not a novice, lest being lifted up with pride he fall into the condemnation of the devil. Moreover he must have a good report of them which are without; lest he fall into reproach and the snare of the devil.

Likewise must the deacons be grave, not doubletongued, not given to much wine, not greedy of filthy lucre; Holding the mystery of the faith in a pure conscience. And let these also first be proved; then let them use the office of a deacon, being found blameless. Even so must their wives be grave, not slanderers, sober, faithful in all things. Let the deacons be the husbands of one wife, ruling their children and their own houses well. For they that have used the office of a deacon well purchase to themselves a good degree, and great boldness in the faith which is in Christ Jesus.
I Timothy 3:1-13

The "likewise" in the transition from the qualifications of pastors to those of deacons suggests that what applies to pastors also applies to deacons. Therefore, I suggest that it is acceptable for a man to desire the office of a deacon, because in so doing he desires a good work. However, the deacon must be sincere in his motive. There is nothing wrong in a man saying, "I'd like to be a deacon someday," but he ought to be sincere in that position, and make an effort to fulfill his Scriptural duties and responsibilities selflessly, as unto the Lord, not to get a "position" to satisfy his own pride.

He ought to be consistent. In other words, his language at Sunday school ought to be his language at work. His attitude in a deacons meeting ought to be the same as in a business meeting. His attitude in the pastor's presence ought to be consistent with the rest of his life. There must be consistency in his life.

First Timothy 3:8 also tells us that a deacon is to abstain from alcohol.

He must not be miserly with his possessions. He is to be an example of giving. That does not necessarily mean that he has to give away everything—unless Jesus wants him to. Some men have given everything, but they could not out-give God.

The deacon must believe the gospel without wavering, "holding the mystery of the faith in a pure conscience." The gospel gives us freedom from the bondage of the law, a standard no one can live up to. We are now free from the law to serve Christ in the power of the Spirit. We need to realize that the gospel does grant us liberty but not a license to collaborate with the enemy. We need to believe the gospel without wavering. We must live like redeemed people.

Deacons must be approved by the pastor. "Let these also first be proved" does not define by whom they are proved, but, logically, that must include both the pastor and the congregation. The congregation will vote as a means of expressing approval. If the pastor cannot approve of them as serving and working with him, then there is an automatic conflict. There should be no conflict in the work of God. The deacons must be men who are proven by experience.

He is to be blameless in character (I Timothy 4:10). That does not mean he is perfect, but it means that he is not to be blamed because of character flaws in his life. If he is a moldable, spiritual man, once the evidences of character flaws are brought to his attention, he will be willing to take the reproof, admonition, or correction and change those things.

The deacon's family life is important. What you are at home, you are! A wife plays an important part in a man's life and in his ministry. The deacon is to be the husband of one wife. We need to emphasize his relationship to his wife and their spiritual relationship. The deacon's wife, like her husband, must be sincere, not a gossip, not giggly or giddy, but polite and ladylike, faithful in all things (I Timothy 3:11). The deacon must rule his children with consistent, appropriate, loving discipline. His children need to be well disciplined.

Deacons are to be bold in the faith—not only full of faith (said of Stephen in Acts 6:5), but also bold in the faith (I Timothy 3:13). Boldness comes through Holy Spirit power. As a man steps out in faith and does what God commands, he sees God bless and provide. Seeing how God blesses obedience brings great confidence, not in one's self, but in God.

The final qualification takes us back to motive: do it all for Christ Jesus. The service of a deacon is all done for the faith which is in Christ Jesus. Serve your pastor because of your love for Christ, not just your admiration for the pastor. Let all you do be for Christ Jesus.

A SUMMARY AND APPLICATION

Salvation

The first point may seem elementary, but it is important: his salvation testimony must be clear. By that I mean he must be able to give a ready testimony of the hope that is within him. If a man does not know when he was saved or cannot tell you about how he was saved, he probably is not saved. That man certainly ought not to fill the office of a deacon. I have seen churches with men who served as deacons who could not tell you any reason for their selection except for the fact that the church asked them to fill that position. Biblical qualifications, including a clear testimony of salvation by grace through faith, were not considered.

Second, he must have a life that is consistent with his verbal testimony. The admonition throughout the New Testament is that our conduct agree with our profession. Consistency is absolutely necessary if we are to be usable servants of God.

Third, it is necessary that his wife and family are saved (except of course for the younger children, still coming to the age of understanding) and living consistent Christian lives. This is a thing that many times is overlooked in the selection of personnel in the ministry. There must be an exemplary family relationship because the wife is the other part of the man and the children are a reflection on their home.

Service

The second major area is his service. Although this goes far beyond "church services" as church meetings, he and his family certainly must be regular in attendance at all the events of the church. The Bible says in Hebrews, "Not forsaking the assembling of ourselves together" (10:25). The New Testament church did not necessarily meet at 9:45 a.m., 11:00 a.m. and 7:00 p.m. on Sunday, but I am also sure that, at whatever times they met, the deacons were there. The following services are important for deacons to attend:

- Sunday school, in which we impart Bible knowledge to our families and those who come under the influence of our church.
- Sunday morning service, which is the inspirational or motivational hour to encourage us in doing the will and work of God. This is often a service with special emphasis on the salvation message.
- Sunday evening service, a time of further teaching, often with a focus on a special topic.
- Wednesday evening prayer service because "men ought always to pray, and not to faint" (Luke 18:1).
- Regular visitation program, although only one part of being a witness for Christ, it makes a public statement of the deacon's commitment to bringing others to Christ.
- All special services, certainly any revival or evangelistic meetings, as much as possible; and weddings and funerals, in the spirit of rejoicing with those who rejoice and weeping with those who weep (Romans 12:15).

The only reason that a deacon should be absent would be sickness or a work schedule that he does not have the power to alter.

Beyond the *church services,* the deacon must also be faithful to any *task of service* that he accepts: he must see that task to completion. The lack of character today in our churches is probably tied directly to the failure of leadership to complete what it attempts. Once we accept a responsibility, we need to stay with it until it is done or until our job description is changed.

This faithfulness in service is not limited to the spiritual arena. As a deacon, a man must be consistent in service as becomes an ambassador for Christ—at church, on the job, and in social contacts. Everywhere he goes there must be consistency in his testimony of faithful service.

Separation

The third major requirement is his *personal* and *ecclesiastical separation*. The deacon must live a life untainted by the sins of this secular world. That is, he must live a life of personal separation. In the first place, he must not smoke or drink alcoholic beverages or condone those who do. He must not attend Hollywood-style movies or even Christian-made movies shown in worldly places such as theaters associated with Hollywood-style movies.

In a recent visit to my former church, a small, country church in the tobacco belt of Tennessee, I was saddened to see a couple of deacons step outside to smoke between Sunday school and the worship service. They have chosen to make a living raising tobacco because of the money involved. Their eyes seem to be blinded to the fact that smoking is wrong, and, therefore, raising tobacco is wrong. Praise the Lord, this source of income is diminishing because even the general population is using less tobacco. Still, these men are responsible for their decision and its impact. One told me, "It's not right, probably, anyway." In America, we know that even lost people who smoke look on Christians with the same habit as hypocrites.

The deacon must dress modestly according to biblical standards. Since I Timothy 3 requires that he be an effective leader of his home, his family must also dress modestly.

The deacon must abstain from social gatherings such as dances and club events where questionable entertainment is present, or parties of a sinful nature which would cause him to lose his testimony. Many today are forced by the very positions that they hold to attend corporate functions that may not be perfectly to their liking, but there is a way that we can retain our Christian testimony in the midst of all of this if we so desire. Yet, there are certain of those functions we absolutely ought not attend, and no company in my experience would make you go if you have a spiritual conviction involved. This can be a place where the faithfulness which must characterize the life of a deacon may be a help. If you have been the best salesman on the force or if you have made more money for the company than anyone else, you can pretty well do as you choose.

Some years ago when I was working as a manager in technical services for a large, national company (*before* my IBM days), a friend and I attended a required seminar together. It seemed to be one of the usual kind, designed to help managers keep their skills sharp. But early in the first meeting, we saw that this was going to be anything but the usual. As the speaker began talking about meditation as a way of dealing with stress in the workplace, my friend looked over at me and said, "Do you know what that is—it's New Age." Sure enough, we soon found that this well-known corporation intended to have all of its employees do-ing yoga-style meditation at a certain hour every day. We approached the director of our department to express our concern. While we were willing to take on any assignment for the company—even the ones no one else wanted—we could not do this. The director knew us as gener-ally cooperative, hard-working people, and he wanted to do whatever he could to keep us on board. As a result, the 85 people in our department were given an option—and, of course, no one opted for yoga! Now, this department director was also a Christian, and he was already sympathetic toward our concerns. But the fact that we both had consistently and effectively done all the work-related duties we were assigned made it easier for him to stand up for our position. All the attributes that make a person a good Christian also make a person a good employee. Respect-ing people—treating them as having value—is basic to management, and the Bible teaches the inestimable value of every person. Every company wants employees who demonstrate the character traits listed as the "fruit of the Spirit" in Galatians 5:22-23. Being a faithful worker lays a solid foundation for the time when you must take your stand.

Finally, there is the ever-present issue of "gray areas," practices that are not clearly right or wrong in the eyes of the deacon, or others. The deacon must be more focused on spiritual goals and biblical prin-ciples than on personal gain or pleasure. This means that the matter of biblical principles is more important than his own personal bias about something. There may be something that is not necessarily sinful for an individual to do, but it would not further the cause of Christ if he did it. Consequently, the deacon should be more interested in preserv-ing biblical principles, presenting the Gospel, and being an example of the faith than in serving his own personal pleasures or personal desires. Therefore, the deacon must live by the polices established for any staff members, paid or unpaid, including the staff of the Christian school, if there is one. This is part of the deacons' being called to live by a higher standard than the average church member.

The more highly you hold your personal standards, the more likely your church will stay biblical for years to come.

Furthermore, the deacon must live a life free from the entanglements of false and compromising religion. This is ecclesiastical separation.

Be ye not unequally yoked together with unbelievers: for what fellowship hath righteousness with unrighteousness? and what communion hath light with darkness? And what concord hath Christ with Belial? or what part hath he that believeth with an infidel? And what agreement hath the temple of God with idols? for ye are the temple of the living God; as God hath said, I will dwell in them, and walk in them; and I will be their God, and they shall be my people. Wherefore come out from among them, and be ye separate, saith the Lord, and touch not the unclean thing; and I will receive you, And will be a Father unto you, and ye shall be my sons and daughters, saith the Lord Almighty.
II Corinthians 6:14-18

Our postmodern society defines "tolerance" as saying that everything is equally true. In the twenty-first century the greatest "evil" is to say that one thing is right, and therefore its opposite must be wrong. The very least we can do for the Lord is to speak the truth in love. We should never cooperate in religious work with those who deny such critical doctrines as the inspiration of Scripture, the deity of Christ, or the necessity of blood atonement. To work alongside them gives weaker brethren the idea that there is no difference, or at least no difference that matters. "Can two walk together, except they be agreed?" (Amos 3:3)

The deacon must believe the fundamentals of the faith. Doctrinal purity is an absolute basic requirement for any leader in the church. Furthermore, every church needs to have a clearly expressed statement of what it believes. That statement of faith should be part of the church's constitution and bylaws.

These two types of separation, personal and ecclesiastical, are related. Before a person goes astray ecclesiastically, he has to go astray personally. Where there is no ecclesiastical separation from modernism and liberalism, you will also find that there is little personal separation from the world. The more highly you hold your personal standards, the more likely your church is to stay biblical for years to come.

THE ELECTION OF DEACONS

One of the most important choices in the local church is the selection of a pastor. The selection of the pastor and, in a larger ministry such as the one I happen to be involved in, his administrative staff, is certainly an important process. However, the next most important issue for the church is the selection of deacons. Additionally, many local churches use the deacons as the pulpit committee to guide the process of selecting a pastor, further emphasizing the importance of having the right men in this position.

The process of selecting deacons varies from ministry to ministry. Once a church is established the process of electing new deacons and their length of service are determined by the constitution of the church. Some churches elect deacons to serve a lifetime; some use a rotating system.

In our church we have a rotating system, where deacons serve three years and then rotate off for a year. After one year, they may be renominated. This allows many men to be involved as deacons.

The following list summarizes the election process at our church:

- Written nominations for the office of deacon shall be submitted by the congregation to the pastor. Nominees must have been members of the church for at least one year.
- The pastor and deacons shall review the nominees and send questionnaires to those who qualify according to the Scriptures (Acts 6 and I Timothy 3). [A copy of the questionnaire used for our ministry is included as an appendix.]
- Qualified men shall complete the questionnaire and return it to the pastor or chairman of deacons to indicate their desire to serve as a deacons.
- The pastor and deacons review the questionnaires and draw up a ballot to be presented to the congregation a minimum of one week prior to the election.
- At a business meeting of the congregation, each voting member may vote for one man for each of the vacancies to be filled. The men receiving the greatest number of votes will fill the vacancies.

- The deacon shall serve a three-year term and shall rotate off for one year before being eligible for reelection.
- It is the goal of the church to have at least seven deacons serving each year. Additional deacons may be added as needed. If seven qualified men are not available to serve, a rotated deacon may be nominated by the pastor and deacons to serve another term. The church may operate with fewer than seven deacons if necessary because of a lack of qualified men willing to serve.
- Nomination and election are to precede the beginning of each fiscal year.
- If, in the opinion of the pastor and the other deacons, a deacon becomes unfit to function, the other deacons shall recommend to the members of the church that said deacon be removed. Matthew 18:15-20 shall be the procedure followed in all such cases. This recommendation shall be presented to the membership of the church, and the majority vote shall be final. A new deacon may be elected to fill this vacancy for the remainder of the unexpired term for which he is elected.
- Full-time employees of the church shall not serve as deacons.
- Deacon vacancies occurring for any reason shall be filled according to regular election procedures except that the election shall be held at a meeting of the members as soon as possible after such vacancies shall occur. The deacon so elected shall hold office for the remainder of the unexpired term for which he is elected.

We always vote by secret ballot. Everyone marks a ballot, and the men receiving the highest number of votes are elected to serve for the next three years.

This is a process that works. It allows the people to choose from among them men who have been nominated by the people, who have been screened by the pastor and deacons, who have expressed the desire to serve, and who are now allowing their names to be on a ballot.

First Deacons in a New Church

The selection of the first deacons in a new church presents some variations on this basic plan. Matt Sanders, a church planter in Caracas, Venezuela, gives us valuable insights on these issues. He is a missionary, but what he says applies to new churches anywhere.

The first question is when to elect the first deacons. The church at Jerusalem did not start off with deacons; they were elected when a need arose. Every church will be different, but Brother Sanders did not see a need for deacons until his church had grown to about 80 people.

Furthermore, the Bible does not mandate the number seven. Remember, the church at Jerusalem was a large, multi-thousand-member church. It also existed in a different time, culture, and economy from ours. The pastor needs to give prayerful consideration to how many men are needed to do the work that needs to be done. He also may be limited by the number of men who have matured enough spiritually to qualify for the position. Brother Sanders started with two deacons. With himself as pastor, that would bring three people into the discussion, enough to make for a good interaction of ideas and views. Having two deacons also established greater accountability one to another.

Special attention must be given to preparing the congregation for the process of selecting first deacons. In any church, this is a time for teaching the biblical principles involved, but all the more in a new work. In Brother Sanders' situation, most of his people came out of a Roman Catholic background, where there was no such position as a deacon. In a way, this makes it easier: whatever he said was taken as the total picture. With this privilege of trust, though, came the responsibility of pointing them back to the Scriptures, encouraging them to be Berean believers, searching the Scriptures daily. They were no longer in a church where priests, popes, and the traditions of men were the authorities. It may be more challenging in a new church in a culture like ours in America. People come from a variety of church backgrounds with a variety of assumptions about what a deacon does. The idea that deacons are servants of the church, not corporate boards, is likely to need teaching. The fact that all the possible errors cannot be anticipated increases the importance of thoroughly teaching all that the Bible says about deacons.

The nomination process is essentially the same. In a new, small church, the fact that there has been a period of time without deacons has a benefit. People know whom the pastor has asked to take on responsibilities like song-leading, organizing and making announcements, or teaching Sunday school. They also know who has been faithful in evangelism and other activities open to all. These factors influence the people's choices of whom to nominate.

After the nominations the pastor must take the responsibility for screening according to Bible standards. Sometimes people will nominate a deacon candidate because they are unaware of something in that person's background, such as divorce. If the pastor has properly taught these standards, he may not need to go to the nominee and tell him that he was nominated but cannot serve because of some unchangeable past event. The nominee should understand. The pastor also does not want to embarrass the nominee publicly, but he may want to say in a generic way before the congregation that people might be nominated but cannot serve because of private matters that are not known to the congregation or because they themselves do not feel that this is the proper time to take on that responsibility. This statement is important to help the one who did the nominating to realize there may be reason that the person he nominated did not end up on the ballot.

Sometimes a nominee is questionable because of less clear-cut issues, such as his degree of involvement or loyalty. Here, the pastor should go to that individual. He should not dodge this responsibility but accept it as an opportunity to minister. In that first election, there was a man nominated who was having problems with his marriage. Brother Sanders went to discuss it with him, in part because he believed that man would be encouraged to know that more than one church member thought that highly of him. He went in a spirit of meekness, explaining his application of the qualifying principles of I Timothy 3 and suggesting that serving as a deacon would not be wise at this time. That church member understood and accepted his pastor's decision. In such a conference it is important to remember Proverbs 15:3: "A soft answer turneth away wrath: but grievous words stir up anger."

It is a scary thing to entrust the selection of first deacons to a new congregation. It would be easy for the pastor to say that he knows best and to appoint his choices. It would be easy, but it would not be right. That is not the pattern of Scripture. If a pastor has taught his people, they know what to do, and they have reached a level of spiritual maturity where they can apply that knowledge. The pastor needs to do his part and then trust the Lord for the results.

THE RESPONSIBILITY TO THE OFFICE

We are in crucial times within the Christian faith. Not so long ago the moral and financial failures among preachers and Christian leaders were making one headline after another, and the lost world mocked. There is no logic to it, but some people will use the sins of men as an excuse to ignore the claims of God. Your sin may disgrace God and hold the door to Hell open for someone. I am reminded of Nathan's charge to David: "Because by this deed thou hast given great occasion to the enemies of the Lord to blaspheme" (II Samuel 2:14).

The office of a deacon is defined very clearly in the Word of God, as is the office of pastor, with very high requirements. If we accept the office of a deacon, we must also be committed to its responsibilities. We, as Christian leaders, have a responsibility to our office.

Once when I was interviewing deacon nominees, a young prospective deacon made this statement: "I just do not feel that I can serve. I am awed by the office of a deacon and the responsibility of it because it is so distinctly defined within the Word of God." That young man was approaching the office of the deacon in the way that it should be approached. I am not saying that holding the office of deacon makes you something special, but I think that the office is important to God and that we have the responsibility to accept this important office as it is defined in Scripture. We must be responsible to the office and not waver from the truth. We are responsible to live up to the standards of the office as described in Acts 6 and I Timothy 3. We are responsible to complete our tasks diligently. My recommendation to anyone who has been elected to the office of deacon is to approach this with a sober and contrite heart, one of humility, and with the attitude of a servant.

Our responsibility is great because of the One who has given it to us. If your church goes through the process of electing deacons in a biblical way, then, I believe, God Himself has given you the responsibility to serve. If the plan of Acts 6 is God's plan—that Sprit-filled members of the church should choose out from among them men full of the Holy Spirit—then this selection process is God's way of putting people into the position of deacons. You have an opportunity given to you by God, and He wants you to be responsible to it.

One of the saddest stories I have heard in recent days shows the importance of a deacon's responsibility. A deacon in a Baptist church knew for 10 years that his pastor was in an immoral relationship, but the deacon did nothing about it. I suppose he was afraid. He felt committed to the church and thought that, if he mentioned the situation, it would split the church. In my opinion, his actions violated his office. He was not being responsible to his office. As it turned out, the situation did come to a head. The immorality was discovered, brought forth, and dealt with. But it was too late. The pastor lost his entire family. I wonder how this would have turned out if it had been dealt with properly and early—only the Lord knows.

My encouragement to you is to be responsible. Determine that you are going to protect the office. Live your life in such a way that you will be seen by God and by other people as one who does his duty diligently. If you notice your fellow deacon not living up to his responsibility, hold him accountable—this is what committed friends do. If his family is not living up to necessary standards, it is your responsibility as a deacon to go to that man in a Christian way and help him work through these issues, making sure the office of deacon is held as one that God will be pleased with, that people outside the church will respect, and that members of the church will have confidence in.

Many people make fun of preachers because of some bad things a few have done. I still recall coworkers at IBM mocking a nationally known religious leader. "Look at those tears in his eyes when he says, 'I have sinned,'" they said. It was good that he confessed his sin, but it sure was sad that it had to come to that. If that leader had been around the right men, serving, helping, loving him—even challenging him if necessary—I wonder if that sin might have been avoided. Our responsibility is to each other, to our office, to our pastors, to our people, and to the Lord. If there are problems, we deal with them. We do not sweep them under the rug. We make sure that people look at our churches and our pastors as organizations or individuals of integrity, truth, and love. If we are responsible, we will play a big part in molding the testimony of our churches in our communities. This is what being responsible to the office of deacon is all about.

If you feel a little overwhelmed at the qualifications and responsibilities of being a deacon, that is not a bad thing. It is not an indication that you are not ready. In fact, it may be an indication that you *should be* a deacon, because you understand the position and take it seriously. Remember that the role of the deacon is ordained by God for the local church, and what God commands, He enables people to do. Along with the calling of God comes His enabling. Along with obedience comes blessing. May the Lord richly bless you as you serve Him, your pastor, and your church.

CHAPTER REVIEW

1. Deacons are not
   - Pastors.
   - Committees.
   - Boards.
2. Deacons are
   - Servants of the church and burden-lifters for the pastor.
   - Examples of the faith.
   - They are witnesses.
   - They may be preachers.
3. The personal requirements for a deacon are as strict as for a pastor:
   - A clear testimony of salvation—in words and in lifestyle.
   - Faithfulness to church services and faithfulness in service to the church.
   - Separation from worldly activities and from false or compromising religion.
   - Clarity in the doctrines of the faith.
4. The election process should reflect the basics of Acts 6:
   - The congregation selects Spirit-filled men.
   - The pastor or pastors assign their tasks.
5. The office of deacon carries a great responsibility and a strict accountability.

You will give account to God: Live Responsibly!

GPS (GETTING THE PRINCIPLES SUMMARIZED)

Find answers to these questions in the chapter.

Deacons Are Not
1. List three things which deacons were not intended to be.
2. How do you reconcile the need for legal functions associated with the board of a nonprofit organization and the fact that the deacons do not rule as a corporate board?

Deacons Are
3. What does the word likewise in 1 Timothy 3:8 suggest?

Origin as a Key to Purpose
4. What is one benefit of the deacon standing up for the pastor's position, even beyond the pastor's doing it?
5. Give three cautions in regard to deacons' defense of their pastor.
6. What two general functions did the first deacons have?
7. What qualifications for deacons are mentioned in Acts 6:3?

A Summary and Application: Service
8. What two reasons are listed as acceptable for a deacon to miss church services?

A Summary and Application: Separation
9. Briefly explain the two types of separation.

First Deacons in a New Church
10. How many deacons should a church have?

APPles (Applying the Principles Practically)

Apply these ideas to your church. Discussion will often go beyond just the facts in the reading.

Origin as a Key to Purpose

1. What is the author's theory of how deacons came to be ruling bodies in some American churches?

2. "The operational standard of a local church is different from that of an ordinary business." Discuss the contrasts between money-first decisions, financially irresponsible decisions, and wise financial decisions.

A Summary and Application: Salvation

3. How does the requirement of salvation (as qualification for the office of deacon) go beyond the verbal testimony?

A Summary and Application: Service

4. Although the text states that "service" is much more than going to "church services," it states that a deacon should not miss services if he can help it. Can a deacon attend everything? Defend your answer. If you do not believe a deacon must attend everything, list the services which he must not miss.

First Deacons in a New Church

5. What are some of the problems that can arise in the nomination of deacons, and how may they be addressed?

THE WORK OF A DEACON

For they that have used the office of a deacon well purchase to themselves a good degree, and great boldness in the faith which is in Christ Jesus.
I Timothy 3:13

Consider that phrase from I Timothy 3:13—"they that have *used* the office of a deacon."The role of deacon is not an ornament to wear: it is a job to do. Sometimes people in the world—or worldly people in the church—talk as if being a deacon was like being an officer in the military, some sort of rank or honor. Granted, it is an honor any time God calls any of us to do any task for Him, but the deacon is honored to be the "servant of all" (Matthew 10:44).

A TRUE-TO-LIFE APPLICATION: NO "YES-MEN" HERE

He was my friend. We worked side by side on church workdays, sang in a quartet together, and we each had a son on the school's soccer team. But I could see that he had a burr under his saddle. It began with what he considered to be an unwise expenditure for new furniture in the church office. He brought his question to the pastor, as he should, and then to the deacons. When the decision did not go his way, he just would not let it go. Every time I was with him, he had an ever-growing list of criticisms. At first they were all about how that money could have been better used, but the circle of criticisms grew ever wider. When I urged him to let the matter go, his response was, "You deacons are just a bunch of 'yes-men' doing what the pastor tells you to do." How are "supporting your pastor" and "being a 'yes-man'" different? And how can you restore such a hurting—and hurtful—brother?

THE SCRIPTURAL FRAMEWORK

The specific set of duties to be performed by the first deacons is given to us in Acts 6:1-7. In that situation, it was described as "waiting on tables." I believe this passage not only teaches the basic reason for which deacons exist but also indicates the broad applications that may be made to their role. The role of deacons is to serve the people, doing tasks that someone other than the pastor can do. ("It is not reason that we should leave the word of God, and serve tables.") This service, then, frees the pastor to do that which is his specific role. ("But we will give ourselves continually to prayer, and to the ministry of the word.") The very specific nature of their job does not mean that all that the deacons ever did was to take care of the meal ministry for widows. Rather, it suggests how specific the assignments may be. It is the job of the deacon to do whatever he can to free up the pastor to do whatever he must.

The source of the deacons' duties is very important. In Acts 6:3 the apostles speak of the first deacons as men "whom we may appoint over this business." The deacon is to be appointed to his duties by the pastor. Those duties, unless appointed, are not duties at all. In other words, he is to be used, and that is completely scriptural. Deacons are servants of the church and servants of the pastor. They serve the pastor by serving the people of the church.

The Bible goes on to say much about what kind of people these first deacons were. It also mentions some of the awesome things they did. Stephen was a bold witness, proclaiming the message of the Messiah to "the council" and the high priest, probably the same desperate men who had recently been responsible for the Crucifixion of Christ. Stephen was martyred, and, in the persecution that followed, the church was scattered, and "they that were scattered abroad went every where preaching the word" (Acts 8:4). After this dispersion, we see the deacon Philip deeply involved in an evangelistic campaign in the city of Samaria, north of Jerusalem. Then we find the Holy Spirit directing Philip south of Jerusalem to evangelize an Ethiopian official "of great authority."

In Acts 8:36, we find that, in the absence of an ordained pastor, a deacon may baptize. After the Ethiopian official placed his faith in Christ, Philip baptized him, and the new convert went on his way back to his own land rejoicing. If there is not an ordained pastor present, the church may vote (putting this in the context of modern church organization) for a deacon to baptize people who are ready for this first step of obedience after salvation. This baptism is just as valid as if a pastor baptized.

The scriptural framework is clear: the deacons are to be men approved by their peers in the church and appointed by their pastor to serve the church.

AN ORGANIZATIONAL APPLICATION

Yet, for all of the things we know that certain deacons did, and for all that is said in two major passages about the spiritual and character requirements of deacons (Acts 6 and I Timothy 3), not much is said about the specific day-by-day tasks of deacons. I believe that this is because God intends that these specific tasks should be adaptable to different churches' needs, as long as they fit within the framework of serving the pastor by serving the people. Therefore, in addition to meeting the spiritual requirements for the office (what a deacon *is*), deacons must be faithful in fulfilling those duties appointed by the pastor (what a deacon *does*).

Our ministry is to people, no matter who they are. It is to serve, not to be served.

The following framework suggests an application of this principle of service to our twenty-first century churches. It is not the only way it can work, but it has proven workable for us at one local church, and is easily adaptable to other churches and their specific needs.

Duties of All Deacons

The term "deacon" suggests the idea of a helper—a helper to the pastor in doing the work of the Lord. The responsibilities of witnessing, of teaching, and of caring for the weak, the lame, the old, the widow, the orphans—all of these are responsibilities and duties that were specifically given in the Bible. Because they were so given, these duties are especially important. Deacons may be charged with the following:

1. Duties and ministries of the church as assigned by the pastor.
2. Care of the needy.
3. Care of the widows and fatherless. Each deacon should be assigned a widow for himself and his family to care for in a special way.

4. Preparation and oversight of the Lord's Supper and baptismal services.
5. Meeting regularly with the pastor. This meeting, monthly or more often if needed, allows the deacons to give the pastor insights from a layman's standpoint on spiritual matters of the church. This does not provide dictatorial power to the deacons. Instead, it provides for the pastor both wisdom from a "multitude of counselors" and a point of accountability.
6. Duties related to church discipline.
7. Yearly review of the budget. The deacons play a major role in developing the budget and approving it for presentation to the congregation.
8. Peacemaking. Every deacon should have as a primary goal the maintenance of scriptural unity among the members of the church.
9. Helping. Wherever a deacon sees a need, he should give his help. While no one can—or should—do everything, the kind of person who should be a deacon will naturally be among the most willing.

Deacons should make themselves available to their pastor at all times to help solve problems. Many of the problems which come his way could be handled by a deacon.

Legitimate problems do not usually go away by themselves; they must be resolved. The first step to solving a problem is to define what the problem is. The problem definition phase is critical: too easily we can hastily implement a "solution" which does not really meet the real need, because often there is a deeper need, for which the immediate need is only a symptom. Doctors sometimes call it the "presenting problem." A patient may come in with a problem such as fatigue, but the fatigue may represent a deeper need, like a problem with the thyroid or heart. Problems are defined by listening with an open mind. Once the problem is defined, the next step is to see who has been affected. The third is to develop possible resolutions. The problem definition and potential resolutions should be bathed in prayer. Our natural tendency is to resolve the problem as we see it without truly understanding what the problem is. We may solve the problem as it affects us without realizing who else has been affected.

Because change is never easy, deacons must be willing to patiently, lovingly persuade people. Sometimes it is enough to acknowledge to someone that you understand how a change is not desirable for him or her individually, while explaining why it is necessary for the ministry overall. Everyone counts. No one is expendable. If you love people, it will show, and people are more willing to accept change, even at a loss to themselves, if they know they are loved.

Duties of Specific Offices

Within thirty days after the election of deacons, the following officers should be elected: chairman, vice-chairman, and secretary. The officers hold these positions for a period of one year or until their successors are elected.

1. Duties of the chairman

The chairman shall preside over the meetings and oversee the actions of the deacons. He shall meet regularly with the pastor, be informed of the operation of the ministry, and be considered a welcome participant in all staff meetings. For purposes of fulfilling requirements of the state in regard to the church as a 501(c)(3) not-for-profit corporation, he shall serve as the chairman of the corporation's board and be responsible to the people of the church as such.

2. Duties of the vice chairman

The vice chairman shall perform all the duties of the chairman of the deacons in the chairman's absence or in the inability of the chairman to act.

3. Duties of the secretary

The secretary of the deacons shall make and preserve a record of the minutes of all meetings and actions of the deacons. He shall issue notices to the deacons of all upcoming meetings.

4. Duties of the treasurer

The treasurer is responsible for financial records and reports. He takes responsibility for securing the offerings, examining the check register, reviewing expense reports of the staff, and securing annual audits.

Duties of Committees

As in any organization, it is important that organizational structures and job descriptions are defined in order for everyone to function in the appropriate manner. Many churches will also organize committees. One such committee may be a "trustee" organization to fulfill the requirements of their particular state. Various other committees may be organized. It is very important that all offices of the local church be in line with the scriptural framework. Since there are only two offices defined in Scripture, pastor and deacon, everything should function within their descriptions.

Each committee should have a job description. Each committee must have a chairman and other deacons who feel led to serve in the area served by that committee. The organization of these committees should be precise and defined well enough so that the deacons can function in an orderly manner and be consistent from one year's deacons to the next.

In our church we have seven committees. These committees, made up of deacons, are appointed at the beginning of each year and serve for one year.

1. Baptism Committee

This committee is responsible for preparing the robes and otherwise assisting in the baptism service.

2. Building Committee

This committee is responsible for the care of the building. When new construction is needed, they advise, approve, and monitor progress of the building.

3. Finance Committee

This committee is responsible for developing the financial guidelines for the church. The members work with the business office to formulate the budget and present it to all the deacons for their approval and subsequent presentation to the congregation for a vote on their approval. The chairman of deacons, the vice chair, the secretary, and the treasurer are automatically members of the finance committee, and one or two other deacons may be appointed to the committee by the chairman.

4. Lord's Supper Committee

This committee is responsible for preparing and serving the Lord's Supper. They are responsible for making sure it is organized in an appropriate fashion so that everything is done decently and in order. Finally, they take care of cleaning up afterward.

5. Missions Committee

This committee is responsible for staying in touch with all the missionaries, making sure that all the missionaries' needs are presented to the church and met, to whatever degree their church can meet those needs. They should visit the mission field from time to time. They must be men whose hearts are focused on missions.

6. New Members Committee

This committee focuses on explaining to new members specific details about the church, answering questions about the church, working with new members' fellowship opportunities, and visiting new members through hospitality programs and other means.

7. Special Needs Committee

This committee focuses on special needs that may arise in the church. Particularly, this includes financial crises or ongoing needs that individual church members may face. Sometimes people outside the church, whether living in the community or just passing through, may look to a church in a time of need. A church should have policies in place to help with such needs in a consistent and compassionate, yet responsible, way.

Even with all this about committees and job descriptions, we must keep the original focus: serving God by serving people. Deacons must realize that, after all, their ministry is to people, no matter who they are, no matter what their condition. Their ministry is to help, not to be helped. It is to serve, not to be served.

Let there never be favoritism. "My brethren, have not the faith of our Lord Jesus Christ, the Lord of glory, with respect of persons" (James 2:1). The church must not cater to people who have money in some hope that their money will benefit the church. We must reach people and help them. Granted, sometimes when people let God straighten out their lives, the result of turning from sins and developing Christian character is an elevation of their standard of living. If they learn to give, this will help the church. But do not get it backwards. Sometimes we seek to "help" people with money so that *we* might be helped, when we ought to meet needs in people's lives and leave the rest to God. Our church is not here to be built; our church is here to build people and to build character. "Seek ye first the kingdom of God, and his righteousness; and all these things shall be added unto you" (Matthew 6:33).

On the other side of the figurative coin is the pride of some who give, compared to the humility of the forgiven saint. If I hear somebody say, "Boy, you don't know how much money I've given to that church," I have very little respect for that man. But if I hear somebody else say, "Man, you wouldn't believe what that church has done for me," I can pretty well tell that fellow has gone to church for the right reason. He has not gone to exhibit his ability to give; he has gone to get what God wants to give him.

The Deacons Meeting

The meeting process is important. As such, it is worthy of the time and effort required to produce an organized meeting. It is also true that a well organized meeting will more likely be esteemed as important. It works both ways. If it is important, we will organize; and if we organize, the participants will believe that it is important.

The attitudes the deacons bring to the meeting are also very important. Of course, at all times deacons should be praying that the Lord would direct their thoughts and that they would be doing what the Lord wants them to do. They should be focusing on the Lord Jesus Christ in every attitude they might have, every action they might display, every decision they might be involved in making. They should want God's mind on every matter. The deacon must develop a trust for, and a confidence in, his pastor and in his fellow deacons. This attitude is very different from that of the world. I worked in the business world and many times saw people jockeying to position themselves for "success," trying to shine their own armor, trying to toot their own horns. This should never be done by deacons. It will destroy that trust and confidence which should characterize the relationship of the deacons and the pastor. This attitude of trust will extend beyond the deacons meeting. When I have decisions to make, I always, without question, talk to my pastor and to fellow deacons, because I want their godly advice.

The deacons meeting should be regularly scheduled—the first Monday of every month, the first Thursday of every month, etc. At our church the deacons meet once a month. Committees will meet to discuss specific matters at other times apart from the main meeting and then bring issues back to all the deacons at the regular meeting. For example, the finance committee would review the budget and bring a recommended budget back to the whole group. All the deacons would then vote on whether to recommend the budget to the church. The church would then vote to approve or disapprove the budget. These meetings, whether of committees or of the whole group, are important. A deacon should be determined that he is going to be there. No matter what might interfere, he should try his best to be there. A deacon must be faithful to his office.

The meeting must have an agenda. Never have a meeting without a plan. It has been said in the business world that, when you are having a meeting, there will be an agenda. Preferably, the organizer of the meeting will develop the agenda. In the positive sense, this is the planned list of matters to consider. However, if there is no plan, it is likely that everyone will come in with his own agenda, in the negative sense: sets of pet peeves and possibly selfish goals. In the latter case, items might come up that are not ready for discussion. It is very important, from an organizational standpoint, that there be a published agenda. The pastor, along with the chairman of deacons, should have the responsibility of putting the agenda together. If other deacons have items to be discussed, they may request that these be planned into the agenda. At the beginning of the meeting, deacons may also request that items be added to the agenda. This is a simple, but very important, process.

The agenda lists both old and new business. The old business involves items that have been previously discussed but are still in progress. This is a time of review—looking at things that have been accomplished and discussing how things are working out in certain situations. Remember to praise God for all His blessings and direction in the church. New business consists of items that need to be dealt with promptly and other situations or issues that need to be prayed about and discussed in future meetings. A sample agenda is provided as an appendix.

At the beginning of the year, each deacon should be equipped with a deacon notebook. This notebook should have division pages for each month. The three-ring binder should be large enough to hold all the information associated with the meetings. The agenda for each month should be kept in that deacon notebook.

The meeting should begin with a time of devotions and prayer brought by a deacon. The deacons each take a turn in leading devotions. The assigned deacon should come prepared to bring encouragement or a challenge to the deacons. I can remember many sessions in which the Bible instruction given by a deacon or by our pastor has been an encouragement to all. I will always remember a session done by one of our deacons on legalism. It was an exhaustive study on what legalism is and the attitudes associated with it. It has helped me for many, many years as I have interacted with people, trying to be careful that I do not become Pharisaical and unrighteously judge other people. Devotions time is very important.

Following the devotional challenge, there should be a time of concentrated prayer. Our meetings start at 7:30 p.m. Many times the devotional and prayer time continues until 9:30 p.m. We have sought God's will, prayed for each other, and prayed for the needs of the church. These are special times in my life that cause me to look forward to the deacons meeting.

Next, the minutes of the last meeting should be read. Then the agenda should be overviewed.

Then, of course, each item must be dealt with. During the meeting, the pastor is the facilitator for the meeting. He will bring up the items and control the agenda. As items are discussed, the pastor should go around the room, making sure everyone provides input. This does not have to be done in an orderly fashion; it may be done just by saying, "What do you guys think about that?" Sometimes we will merely go around the room and seek input from everyone. I have seen many meetings where we would be headed in a certain direction until one man expresses his thoughts and the whole discussion takes a completely different direction. With the prayerful input of all, we could see unity of thought and spirit leading to a decision that would be pleasing to God.

The meeting is a time for discussion, for counsel, for giving advice, for listening, for speaking out, for being frank and honest with one another. Each deacon must participate, but in a balanced way. No one should hold back in false humility or bitter silence. God calls deacons to help the pastor and the church, to bring about unity, and to cause things to be done decently and in order. Eveyone's input is important. However, one deacon should not over-participate to dominate the thinking of other people. There must be a respect for other peoples' opinions.

Deacons should be team players; they must want to discern God's will more than they want to get their own way. With that attitude, godly counsel will be produced.

Duties in Church Discipline

Deacons play a key role in church discipline. We must remember that the real reason for church discipline is not to purge unwanted people, but rather to restore a brother or sister to a right relationship with God and his or her church family. Therefore, it will most likely become the responsibility of the pastor and a deacon to confront a member of the church for discipline and restoration. This process is defined in Matthew chapter 18, and is explored in chapter ten of this book.

I once had to deal with a church discipline problem that involved an individual who had become truly bitter toward our pastor and was spreading discord among the flock. The situation had gotten to the point where all logic had ceased, and the individual had become so vindictive that he was even telling lies. These lies were an outright attempt to destroy the credibility of the pastor and the deacons. The deacons were being accused of being "yes men" to the pastor. When these personal attacks come from a friend in the ministry, someone you respect personally and agree with philosophically, it is hard to understand how these things could be. Any root of bitterness can be confessed and forgiven, but getting people to see and admit their wrong is always the hard part. After this individual rejected several attempts at reconciliation and would not stop spreading discord, church discipline was applied and he was removed from the membership of the church.

When these situations come, then one or more deacons may be called upon to make a visit with the pastor to fulfill the Scriptural obligations of confronting people. Here, especially, the deacon must be sober, serious, and not double-tongued. It is a serious matter when an individual becomes bitter. The deacon must do everything he can as a Christian brother and a leader in the church to confront an individual and to help the individual be restored. Prior to a visit of this nature, the deacon must first of all be prayed up. He must have a pure heart. Perhaps this is why the spiritual qualifications for deacons are essentially the same as for pastors.

The deacon must also have an open mind. He must be determined to listen and to try to understand the situation. Sometimes further investigation is required to fully understand the problem or the perspectives of all involved. Never rush to judgment. Remember, the motive is to restore a brother, not to destroy. Restoration takes time.

When someone is confronted with something that is wrong, he or she must be convinced to change. Change is only possible when the problem is acknowledged. If it is a shortcoming, such as inadequate supervision on a youth group trip, it should be acknowledged as such with specific plans for remedy. If the issue is a sin problem, it must be acknowledged as sin, and there must be willingness to change.

In a former church, I was confronted with a situation in which the chairman of the deacons had an immoral relationship with the church pianist. He acknowledged the sin, admitted that it was wrong, and confessed his sin before God, but he was unwilling to stop his divorce from his wife and dissolve the relationship with the other person. He said, "I have already gone too far." We were unable to convince him that, even though he had been immoral with the other woman, he was still obligated to his wife. As it turned out, two divorces took place. The pianist's husband was a young preacher, so his ministry was marred. All of this came just because someone was not willing to change. True confession and true repentance bring change and a willingness to do right. If we are not willing to do what is right in a situation, we have not repented.

Remember there is no such thing as being restored into the fellowship of the church without true repentance before God. Therefore, we need God's help and discernment. We must articulate to individuals whom we confront that God restores only on the basis of confession of, and repentance from, sin. We must be persistent and persuasive, but, even more, we must pray for the Holy Spirit's working in hearts.

Certain situations require privacy. Sin can never be covered, in the sense of hidden, because "He that covereth his sins shall not prosper: but whoso confesseth and forsaketh them shall have mercy" (Proverbs 28:13). Yet, there are times when privacy must be maintained. The balance is simple. The circle of confession is only as wide as the circle of transgression. If I am angry at you momentarily, and no one but God and I know it, I must confess this to God alone. If I am angry at you and you know it, I must confess it to God and to you. If, however, I am angry at you and lash out at you in some public place or spread gossip, I may need to confess it to the church, because I have marred the testimony of the whole church.

Duties in Relationship to the Pastor

The first responsibility of deacons was related to murmuring in the church—griping and complaining, to put it in modern words. Seven deacons were called upon to help fix the problem so that the murmuring would stop. While murmuring is never right, it might reveal a real need. In Acts 6 certain widows were being neglected. Certainly, a basic biblical reason for being a deacon is to bring unity in the church by solving legitimate problems and, in doing so, to help the pastor be more effective in the ministry of the Word of God and prayer.

Often, however, in this sinful world, the murmuring originates in pride and goes on to gossip or attack. The job of the deacon is also to defend the pastor. The deacon must be willing to speak up for the pastor so that the pastor's image is not distorted. The deacon should be willing to take some direct pressure upon himself to protect his pastor. He should take the more difficult role of one pointing out sin, so that the pastor can be the rescuer, bringing the straying one back into the fold.

Should a deacon be always seen as supporting his pastor? That is, at least, the starting point. The unity of the early church, as recorded in Acts, is clear and distinctive. There is never an excuse to spread discord among the flock. God desires unity. There may be things we disagree on; however, as long as these are not matters of biblical right and wrong, we must agree to disagree agreeably and to not spread discord among the flock. If there ever is an accusation against the pastor on some point of biblical importance, a good answer is "I can't believe that. Come with me, and let's talk to the pastor about that." Very few of the gossips and complainers will be willing to do that. This offer to the accuser, however, sets the stage for the deacon's next step. If that person is not willing to go to the pastor, the deacon must inform the pastor so that the pastor may take the initiative. Bitterness and gossip must not be left to fester and spread. If dealing with them is uncomfortable, letting them go leads to much more difficult problems, and these problems usually are quick to come.

Another reality, though, is that an accusation may be based on a real problem. The first rule to remember is from I Timothy: "Against an elder receive not an accusation, but before two or three witnesses.

Them that sin rebuke before all, that others also may fear" (19-20). Never jump to conclusions, but never shrink from dealing with a matter. Always deal in love, but always seek the truth. The deacon must love his pastor, but he must love the Lord and His church more. Helping a pastor see and deal with a need in his own life may be the most loving thing a deacon can do.

True repentance brings restoration, but failure to forgive is a terrible thing. Carnal people who have been hurt are not willing to forgive. "I can forgive, but I cannot forget" may seem true, but it disguises a lie. Forgiveness is a choice, a choice that we will not bring up a forgiven sin either to the offender or to others, and that we will not allow our own thoughts to dwell on the matter. Remembering lessons learned should bring harmony, not splits. A church split means that people have not forgiven each other. Separation should only come because of differences in doctrinal issues.

The deacon must be willing to confront his pastor for the sake of the ministry. This could be the most difficult thing a deacon is ever asked to do—to confront his pastor and to lead the church in doing what is right. There are situations in which a pastor, having violated his office, could not be allowed to continue as a pastor. This does not mean that he could not be restored to a right fellowship with God and continue to serve God. But to be in the role of a pastor, a man must be "blameless" (Titus 1:6). This word does not mean sinless, certainly, for "all have sinned" (Romans 3:23). Instead, the word "blameless" means that, when that pastor is mentioned, some incident of sin is not the first thing in people's thoughts.

On the other hand, a pastor must be willing to confront even the chairman of his deacons for the sake of the body of Christ. Sin must never be covered.

The deacon is servant of all. To be a deacon means to put others first, to take the hard and unpleasant tasks, and to do it all without expecting appreciation from people here on earth. But that is where the joy is; there is joy in serving Jesus.

CHAPTER REVIEW

1. Deacons are men approved by their peers and called to be servants of the church.
   - They serve the people by meeting needs.
   - They serve the pastor by freeing him up to do his specific, God-ordained tasks.
   - They serve the Lord by demonstrating the beauty of His plan with a Christlike spirit.
2. Some duties apply to all deacons, and all deacons should be incorporated into specialized committees to meet specific needs. Three possible offices:
   - Chairman
   - Vice chairman
   - Secretary
3. Seven possible committees:
   - Baptism committee
   - Building Committee
   - Finance Committee
   - Lord's Supper Committee
   - Missions Committee
   - New Members Committee
   - Special Needs Committee
4. Characteristics of a good deacons meeting
   - Regular occurrence
   - Organization—the agenda
   - Devotions and prayer
   - Reading of the minutes from the last meeting
   - Overview of agenda for the current meeting
   - Each deacon feeling free to give input on each item
5. Deacons must be ready to help in church discipline.
6. Deacons must protect their pastor, yet be willing and able to confront their pastor if necessary.
7. Deacons must welcome and respond correctly if their pastor must confront them.

There is joy in serving God: Work and rejoice!

GPS (Getting the Principles Summarized)

Find answers to these questions in the chapter.

The Scriptural Framework
1. Who approves deacons and who appoints them to their duties? (Acts 6:1-7)

Duties of All Deacons
2. List the three steps of problem solving.
3. What might make people more accepting of a solution which is not all that they wanted?

Duties of Specific Offices
4. Briefly summarize the duties of the chairman, vice chairman, secretary, and treasurer.

The Deacons Meeting
5. Give one practical suggestion to help all involved to consider the deacons meeting as important?
6. What way do the authors suggest starting a meeting?
7. Who leads the meeting?

 APPles (Applying the Principles Practically)

Apply these ideas to your church. Discussion will often go beyond just the facts in the reading.

Duties of All Deacons
1. In the three steps of problem solving, what do you see as most critical or the place where things can most easily go wrong?

The Deacons Meeting
2. How should you handle matters which are not on the already-written agenda for a deacons meeting? Why?

3. What is the difference between being supportive of your pastor and being a "yes man."

Duties in Church Discipline
4. Why is patience part of restoration?

Duties in Relationship to the Pastor
5. What should you do when someone brings an accusation against the pastor to you?

THE PASTOR-DEACON RELATIONSHIP

*Two are better than one; because they have a good reward for their labour. . . .
And if one prevail against him, two shall withstand him; and a threefold cord is
not quickly broken.*
Ecclesiastes 4:9-12

Adversarial or *cooperative*: which adjective best describes the pastor-deacon relationship? I fear the answer is often adversarial, but a cooperative relationship between a pastor and his deacons is essential to the harmony and effectiveness of a local church. Building such a relationship, of course, demands commitment on both sides. Chapter 6 addressed the deacons' commitment to their pastor, but what about a pastor's commitment to his deacons? How can a pastor build a good working relationship with his deacons? The commitment—and sometimes the sacrifice—is great, but the rewards, both here and hereafter, are more than worth it. There are no deeper man-to-man friendships than the camaraderie of ministry, tested under the stress of trial and refined in the fires of adversity.

A TRUE-TO-LIFE APPLICATION: AN AWKWARD MOMENT IN THE CHURCH LOBBY

Imagine yourself as a deacon, fellowshiping in the church lobby on a Sunday evening after the service, and a church member walks up to you. He is obviously unhappy, and he says, "I'm really concerned about the pastor. He seems stuck in a rut, and I wonder if he's been here too long. You're a deacon, and I want to know what you think." What would you say to this person?

A PASTOR'S PERSPECTIVE CARL HERBSTER, PASTOR

Pastors often create many problems for themselves and their churches simply because they imagine that they are the only ones with adequate ministry skills or worthwhile ideas. God has provided pastors and churches with deacons to help bear the weight of responsibility, and a pastor is wise to utilize this provision. In addition to assisting the congregation in many ways, deacons can be a tremendous help to the pastor in the task of perfecting the saints for the work of the ministry. In relating to his deacons, a wise pastor will not only *love* them as brethren, but also *respect* them as counselors, co-laborers, and close friends.

Counselors

The Bible says much about counsel, including some particularly pointed teaching on the subject found in the book of Proverbs. Proverbs 11:14, for example, says, "Where no counsel is, the people fall: but in the multitude of counselors there is safety." Proverbs 13:10 says, "With the well advised is wisdom." Proverbs 12:15 certainly sums up the issue without beating around the bush: "The way of a fool is right in his own eyes: but he that hearkeneth unto counsel is wise." Pastors are no exception to these life principles. A pastor who does not seek and accept godly advice is foolish, but a pastor who "hearkeneth unto counsel is wise."

Deacons should be among a pastor's most-trusted advisors because they can help him discern the Lord's will for the church which they serve together. A wise pastor will not make major decisions or proceed with new programs without the support of his deacons. He will, instead, constantly consult with them about new ideas he has. Sometimes the deacons will reject an idea simply because they are not yet ready for it. Other times, they will recognize that an idea is good but will counsel the pastor not to implement it yet. Or maybe it is just not a good idea. In any case, the pastor should recognize God's leading in the input he receives. In discerning the Lord's will, the timing is as important as the idea itself, and a good idea badly timed may prove disastrous. A pastor who listens to his deacons in these matters will build a strong relationship with these important servants of the Lord. A pastor who rejects his deacons' counsel, on the other hand, will build a wall between himself and a group of men who should be his greatest allies in the ministry.

Co-laborers

In seeking the assistance of his deacons, a pastor should go well beyond accepting their counsel concerning the Lord's will. He should also recognize them as colaborers in actually carrying out the Lord's will in the church. He should give each deacon a place to serve where his unique gifts can be utilized. Having every deacon involved will not only lighten the pastor's load but also will greatly enrich the spiritual life of the congregation.

The fact that each member of the church is uniquely gifted by God means that different people will do things differently. A pastor should not neglect to delegate responsibilities simply because a deacon might not perform a task in precisely the same way that he would. A pastor who trusts his deacons with key leadership positions is showing a confidence in them which will, in turn, build their confidence in him.

Deacons are not "go-fers," but stewards. The go-fer is told to "go for this," or "go do that." He is given only specific, detailed instructions. The steward, as pictured in Matthew 25:14-30, is entrusted with authority to use his discretion as to the best way to get the job done. Of course, this requires wisdom on the part of the deacon too. He does not become a "mini-pastor," running his own church-within-a-church. He also must operate within the boundaries of policy and budget. God still has an orderly system of leadership. There are things a deacon can just do, knowing that the pastor expects them to be done. An example, perhaps, is setting up for the Lord's Supper on the regular schedule. There are things a deacon should do and report to the pastor about, perhaps the counseling of a church member who has brought a complaint or bitterness to that deacon. Finally, there are things that the deacon should check about before doing, perhaps paying a widow's electricity bill in a time of need. The seemingly evident need may be balanced against what the pastor may know about other plans in progress to meet that need, whether there should be some accountability (such as the widow's developing a budget), or other factors. These three levels of decision will be different in every church, and they may change as a deacon and pastor each grow in their understanding of how the other works.

Both the pastor and the deacons must realize, however, that the pastor remains accountable to the Lord, to the deacons, and to the congregation for the work of the ministry. True, he should delegate some responsibilities. When he delegates a responsibility, he must give the authority to get the job done. But he cannot delegate away his accountability for the work of the ministry. That is why the pastor must keep in touch with those who are helping him serve the church. He may not be the doer of everything, but he can supervise. That is also why the deacon who receives the delegated task should remain accountable to his pastor for it, not acting in self-willed independence.

For more on this relationship, see Matt Williams' excellent book, *How to Be a Team Player and Enjoy It: A Study in Staff Relationships*, published by the American Association of Christian Schools. Chapter 2, "The Call to a Relationship," gives good insights on this leader/steward balance.

Communication Helpers

The deacons work more closely with the pastor than most church members. They understand his vision for the ministry as a whole and for its individual parts. They know his love for the Lord and for the people. They also understand his intentions in decisions that have been made or in actions that have been taken. They understand because, often, the deacons were part of the decision-making process. Therefore, they become a front line of communication when people have questions or misunderstandings. Two kinds of communication are involved here.

Sometimes, it is just a matter of communicating information to fill in the details of something going on. There is no ill-feeling or offense, just a desire for some information. The deacon can meet the church member's immediate need and save the pastor time by providing the answers if he has good understanding of the matter.

Sometimes, however, the issue is a criticism of the pastor. Ideally, any church member would go directly to the pastor with such concerns. But this is not an ideal world! The wrong thing to do is for the deacon to listen to the complaint and then to take it to the pastor. The need is for reconciliation between that person and his or her pastor. The deacon's goal is to get the two together, not to relay messages.

A better plan of approach begins with asking, "Have you talked to the pastor about that yourself?"

Too often the response is "Oh, he wouldn't listen to me."

The deacon's response: "Before I talk to him, you need to talk to him about it. If you like, I'll go with you to talk to him." Be careful at this point, that this "going with" is not some distant point in the future, allowing the church member to dump on the deacon now the complaints he or she intended to bring in the first place. The deacon is not going to listen to any complaint until he and the complainer are both with the pastor.

If, however, the person bringing the problem does not accept that offer, the deacon must follow up with a second, more insistent, proposal: "If you do not want to go to the pastor, I'll mention to him that he needs to come and talk to you." Then the deacon should get with the pastor as soon as it is reasonably possible.

However, if the person says that he or she will go to the pastor, the deacon says, "Good. I'll check with Pastor next week to see if he has heard from you."

That follow-up can be very short and simple. The deacon asks the pastor, "Has [name] talked with you about some problem or concern since [the day the issue was brought to the deacon]." If the answer is yes, good. That ends the matter. If not, the deacon simply says, "[Name] has some question or problem. You need to talk to him [or her]."

Pastors and deacons need to support each other. It works both ways. Granted, there will be times when either one is wrong or needs someone else's perspective. However, one of the worst things that can happen is for a deacon to listen to gossip and take up a reproach against his pastor. Churches have been split and people have been hurt simply because of people not knowing how to handle questions and complaints.

Close Friends

A pastor should also see his deacons as close friends. No pastor can afford to cultivate individual friendships at the expense of neglecting other church members, but that does not mean that special friendships will not, or should not, develop. It is both inevitable and appropriate that a special bond will develop between men who pray together, labor together, and share the joys and sorrows of ministry. A pastor should be cautioned not to favor one deacon over the others, but every deacon will naturally be closer to the pastor than the average church member.

This is as it should be. The congregation, after all, chooses deacons to rally behind their pastor and be his companions in ministry.

It is both inevitable and appropriate that a special bond will develop between men who pray together, labor together, and share the joys and sorrows of ministry.

A pastor should never choose a favorite deacon, but sensitive deacons will recognize that a pastor needs one man to whom he can bare his soul. They should choose a chairman from among themselves who can meet this need in addition to fulfilling other duties. By allowing deacons, who are elected by the congregation, to choose a chairman from among themselves, the pastor is essentially allowing the church members to determine who, apart from his wife, will be his closest companion in ministry.

The chairman of the deacons has several unique responsibilities. The pastor should look to that chairman as a confidant. He should expect his input in church discipline and other serious matters. He should keep the chairman informed of everything that is going on in the church, good and bad. After a deacons meeting concludes, the pastor and the chairman always spend some time with just the two together. In this time they have the opportunity to share any observations or burdens with each other, or they can seek counsel one from the other on matters which do not need to be known by the whole group. In this time the chairman can probe deeper and find what the pastor's vision is on any matter. Here, the pastor can share more of his burdens and concerns than even in the deacon's meeting. This time always concludes with the two praying together. Both men must strive to make the relationship one of the highest respect and strictest confidence.

Given the incredibly important role deacons play in his ministry, a pastor's paramount duty to them is to pray for them. First, he ought to pray diligently and fervently for the congregation to choose the right men to serve. Second, he must continually intercede for the deacons he has, asking God to keep them faithful to His Word, to their families, and to their ministries. Such prayer should flow naturally from sincere respect and from the kind of love that "covers a multitude of sins" (Proverbs 10:12), for there will surely be times when both the pastor and deacons, being fallible flesh, will need to seek one another's forgiveness.

A DEACON'S PERSPECTIVE *KEN HOWERTON, DEACON*

Relationships are very important. Our relationship to the Lord is, of course, the most important foundation for the work of being a deacon. On this stands our understanding of being a servant, for we know that God is worthy of the best of our service and that, in serving people, we are ultimately serving God. Furthermore, our relationship to the Lord is the foundation of our attitude toward our pastor, which is also of extreme importance. Every man who serves as a deacon, even before he accepts the position of being a deacon, should search his own heart. Is he entering this relationship with a conscience void of offense, or are there matters he should resolve? Does he love his pastor? Does he have the goal of humbly serving God by helping—truly helping—his pastor in the work of the local church?

Serving as a deacon is a high calling. It comes, often, with the requirement of significant sacrifice. But it also brings great reward, both here and hereafter. It is a beautiful thing to see the work of God going forward as He has designed, despite the challenges of this troubled world. We can be part of this relationship designed by God if we will let God use us. To effectively serve God in the deacon-pastor relationship, we must be committed to a few basic principles on relationships and roles.

Be Faithful

The United States is a wonderful place to live. However, a lack of commitment is epidemic here. It is manifested in the divorce rate, in the lack of follow-through at work, in dishonesty in government, and in the flimsy promises made by some politicians. Many people have no concern for being faithful to anything or anybody. This is something that concerns me, and I am sure that it concerns you. As pastors and deacons, you have an obligation to be faithful to the office to which the Lord has called you. You must be committed to serving the Lord with all your heart, and you must be committed to each other as fellow deacons and as pastor. Most of all, you must be committed to God and be determined in your heart that you are going to be faithful.

Faithful to God

First of all, be determined that you will be faithful to God. Matthew gives a sobering insight about the Lord's return:

Therefore be ye also ready: for in such an hour as ye think not the Son of man cometh. Who then is a faithful and wise servant, whom his lord hath made ruler over his household, to give them meat in due season? Blessed is that servant, whom his lord when he cometh shall find so doing. Verily I say unto you, That he shall make him ruler over all his goods.
Matthew 24:44-47

The apostle Paul was a man who desired very much to be faithful to God. His fear was that he would become a castaway. One of the greatest things that will cause you to be faithful to your Lord is a true fear of the Lord. As a deacon, I fear Him because my job is so distinctly defined in God's Word. With all my heart I want to please God, Who caused me to be elected to the office of deacon.

Faithful to Your Office

Next, be faithful to your office. The office goes beyond you; your faithfulness affects others. Every deacon should be so committed to his position that no one in the church questions whether he takes it seriously. He should be grave, sober, and of a good report (I Timothy 3:1-15), making sure that other men who follow in his footsteps will say, "I'd like to be a deacon one day. I'd like to serve." There is no greater joy than to know that you are leaving a legacy behind, that your life is an example, that you have modeled the way for someone. You must let your light shine so that God is glorified and so that others will see that light and desire to serve as deacons in the days ahead.

Faithful to Your Pastor

Third, you need to be faithful to your pastor. To put that in practical terms, be sensitive to your pastor and his needs, and be ready to act. I Timothy 5:17 tells us that pastors are worthy of double honor. There are many areas that you should be sensitive to.

Be sensitive to his physical needs. If he is sick, you should check on him. If he has a flat tire, you should be willing to fix the flat tire.

Be sensitive to his spiritual needs. You might think it strange that deacons need to be sensitive to the spiritual needs of their pastor. Your pastor has many things pass his way. Pray for him daily. Pray for the Lord to direct him. Pray for protection, wisdom, and Holy Spirit empowerment as he works through many issues in his ministry. Pray for his family that the Lord will protect them and protect their testimony. Encourage him. Find things that you see him doing right. Call him and let him know you notice things that are happening. When times are tough, reassure him that you trust him and have confidence in what he is doing. There have been many times when I have had sessions with the pastor after some issue had to be dealt with in the church. We needed to be an encouragement to each other. In times of trial, trouble, and temptation, find something that you can do to encourage the pastor. Let him know you are supporting him.

Be sensitive to his duties on the Lord's day. If you have some problem that you know about in the church, it would be very unwise to take that problem to him on Sunday morning just before he goes into the pulpit. I would advise you to wait until the end of the day on Sunday night, if possible, or see him after church to discuss the problem. Use discretion in your timing.

Be sensitive of your influence as a helper. Find your area of service and participate in the activities of your church. For example, be an usher, sing in the choir, teach Sunday school. Provide faithful help to your pastor at all times.

Be sensitive to his family's needs. Go beyond what the average church member does in being a blessing to the pastor's family. Encourage them. Provide fellowship. Have them into your home for Sunday lunch. Invite the whole family. Accept the family for who they are, and do not expect perfection. There are many things that pastor's children get blamed for because people have set the wrong expectation of what a pastor's child should be. The pastor's children are going to be children. Also remember that most pastors are fairly dynamic individuals. God has designed pastors to be self-starters and self-motivators, people that can get themselves going, people that can lead. You will often find these same leadership abilities in their children, but without the maturity to express them properly. As you observe those attributes that God has given them, look down the road with understanding. That does not mean, of course, that you should tolerate wrongdoing, but keep a balanced perspective. Support the children, and in so doing, you will establish a relationship with the family. Let them know that you are their friend. Let them know that you are their father's best friend; that you love him and care for him. Let the children know that you love them and care for them.

Be sensitive to the church's attitude toward your pastor. Encourage church members to respect the pastor. There should be times during the year when special recognition is given to the pastor. This causes the congregation to know that you love the pastor and that there is unity in the church. Do not raise him up on a pedestal and cause him to take God's place, but encourage the entire church body to respect him. Encourage the members of the church to respect him individually and create opportunities for the church body to corporately show their love and respect. Good times to do this is are on his birthday, on his and his wife's wedding anniversary, or on the anniversary of his calling to be the pastor of the church.

Be sensitive to his special needs and to his family's life. There are times of need, such as illness, and there are times of joy, such as a child's graduation. You should know those special events. Use these things to build the relationship with your pastor. Let him know that you support him, understand him, and believe that he is God's man. Tell him that. Take these special times to meet needs in a very special way. Beware that you do not worship the pastor, or else people may see him rather than the Lord and the power of God. You should be very sensitive to the fact that you do not lead people to worship a man. There is a balance that must be maintained.

Finally, remember that deacons need to be different and separate from the world. They need to be truly faithful to their office and to be examples of leadership that people will respect. If your pastor is God's man for your church, then convince others by modeling the way.

MAINTAIN THE RELATIONSHIP

Principles Regarding Relationships

Realize that your pastor is not perfect and neither are you. We are imperfect people in an imperfect world trying to serve a perfect God. We need to realize that God accepts us as we are, that He has placed us into our positions of servanthood as deacons or pastors, and that He is patiently helping us grow. We need to realize that we all make mistakes.

Understand your pastor's ministry vision. How can you help your pastor accomplish the unique work of God in your local assembly if you do not deeply understand what your pastor believes that work of God to be? I would recommend to each of you who serve as a deacon that you develop an understanding of your pastor's heart. By that I mean his vision, his goals, and his love for the Lord. Take the time to learn what he is really trying to do, what the Lord is leading him to do. Understanding your pastor at the heart level will create an environment of trust, sharpen your collaboration in ministry, and give you wise answers when others question what your pastor is doing.

Develop trust and confidence. Trust has to do with your beliefs about a person's intentions; confidence deals with your estimation of a person's ability. When you trust your pastor's goals and have confidence in his leadership of the church, then you can begin to have a correct relationship. It is true that one of your roles is to advise your pastor and, perhaps, even to advise him when he needs to reconsider a decision; however, a negative, critical, suspicious attitude never has done the work of God. As new men are elected, lead them in developing this heart relationship, making sure trust and confidence are present.

Be transparent. Let your life be an open book. Let your thoughts be open in deacon meetings. Whenever your pastor asks your advice, you should be be open and frank.

Do not be a "yes man." Do not be a person who just says what he thinks his pastor wants to hear. If you have a different opinion, present your opinion. God has placed you in a position of being a counselor and servant to your pastor because you have something to contribute. If two people agree about everything, one of them isn't necessary!

Your pastor should be one of your best friends. He can be the kind of friend "that sticketh closer than a brother" (Proverbs 18:24), someone on whom you can count for godly counsel and someone with whom you can share anything. When I have decisions to make, I greatly value the wisdom of one who is both my pastor and my friend. Letting the roads of friendship and counsel run both ways between you and your pastor deepens the mutual trust and confidence, and therefore, magnifies the effectiveness of your ministry together.

Principles Regarding Roles

Differences in roles and skills are valuable. A key issue to remember in this relationship is that you as a deacon or as a pastor of a church have different gifts. We bring different skills to the table. It is like a baseball game. Someone has to be the pitcher; someone has to play first, second, or third; someone has to be in the infield; someone has to play in the outfield. Each man must do his job to the best of his ability if the team is going to do well. We each must realize the unique position we have and fulfill our roles to the best of our ability. We also must realize the positions of others and honor them.

If you are a deacon, do not try to be the pastor. The Lord did not call you to be the pastor. The Lord called you to be a deacon. Do not try to be something that you are not. If the Lord has given you the office of deacon, perhaps to serve on the missions committee, then take that position and do the best job that you can. Be a team player. That is what serving is all about. Corporate advisors think that they have discovered something when they talk about building a team, but God was the first team builder. Consider what happened in the New Testament church in the book of Acts. These new Christians sold everything and brought it together; they had all things common, and they worked together. This should challenge us to work together, yet with each fulfilling his specific role. Incredible ministry power proceeds from the selfless application of God's dynamic balance of unity of purpose and diversity of gifts and roles.

God has always had specific roles for specific people. In Acts 13 we read about a thriving church at Antioch. The Holy Spirit said, "Separate me Barnabas and Saul for the work whereunto I have called them." Many churches were started throughout Asia Minor and Europe because everyone was working together for a common goal. Realize that this is what teamwork is designed to do. That is what being a deacon is all about. Find your place and fill it.

Relationship Thoughts from a Wedding

As I attended a wedding while writing an early draft of these thoughts, I was reminded once again of Christ's love for the church. Christ was committed to give His life as a ransom for all. Nothing—no person, no situation, no circumstance—was going to change His determination to stay on the course toward the cross where He would suffer and die for me and my sin. As I witnessed this wedding, I prayed that this couple would have that same love one toward another and truly be committed until death. As I listened to my pastor challenge the young couple, I was truly thankful for God's leadership in my life, placing me where He wants me to serve. I know I have truly been placed into a position of servanthood as a deacon of my church. My pastor relayed to this beautiful young couple that every day will not be as wonderful as this day. There will be disagreements; there will be hurt feelings; there will be misunderstandings; there will be mistakes! However, they should be committed to each other and not allow anything to come between them.

As the wedding ceremony progressed, my mind drifted over some events of the last few months, some of the busiest of my life. That summer had been a wonderful and blessed time for my family. My two sons, who both made professions of faith between the ages of five and seven, now in their later teens had come to a true, saving knowledge of Christ. One had been serving as a counselor at the Wilds of the Rockies, a Christian camp, and the other had been a camper under the preaching of Mike Manor. What a great summer! Both were to be baptized the next Sunday night by my pastor and friend, Dr. Carl Herbster.

Blessings always come after testings, and testings after blessings. Shortly before this time, I had been deeply involved in helping a family through some problems involving their child and the Christian school which is part of our church. These problems could have strained relationships with Pastor and the school staff, but I was determined, by the grace of God, to keep relationships right.

As this young bride and groom were being challenged concerning their commitment to each other, I was reminded of my commitment to the cause of Christ and to the office of a deacon.

The relationships I have with the pastor, staff, and fellow deacons are very important and require the same kind of determination and commitment that Christ has. The mutual commitment of Christ and the church is pictured in the wedding vows, and, during that wedding, tears began to fill my eyes as this truth from God established itself in my heart and soul. Therefore, I was and am resolved that nothing—no person, no situation, no circumstance—is going to interfere, even in a very small way, with my commitment to maintain these pastor-deacon relationships.

I have spent many hours writing my thoughts in preparation for a book that I pray will help other men who might desire to serve as deacons. This book is also written to young preachers who feel led into the pastoral ministry. I hope that this book will provide some insight for right relationships with the deacons that will serve with them in a local New Testament church.

Gentlemen, this relationship goes beyond us. It is commanded by God. We must be committed that we will not allow anything to destroy this relationship. The same kind of commitment we have to our wives and to Jesus Christ must be applied to this relationship also. Deacons, though some staff member or fellow deacon hurt you, love that person anyway. Though your pastor makes a mistake that hits close to home, love him anyway. Pastor, though some deacon hurts you or lets you down, love him anyway. Being a servant goes beyond us and our feelings. Do not let anything destroy the relationship you had when you were called and elected to your office or position. When the devil attacks, do not give up. Fight back.

Enjoy and endeavor to preserve the divinely ordained pastor-deacon relationship. It is a privilege and a joy to labor together in unity, and you have a good reward for your labor.

CHAPTER REVIEW

From the Pastor's Perspective

1. Deacons can and should be a pastor's closest friends and strongest allies in the ministry.
2. Deacons are, for the pastor ...
   - Counselors: In the multitude of counselors there is safety.
   - Co-laborers: Trust each other.
   - Communicators: If there is a complaint, the deacon brings together the person with the complaint and the pastor for the purpose of reconciliation.
   - Close friends: Don't play favorites, but cultivate relationships with those the Lord brings to labor at your side.
3. The pastor must pray for the deacons.

From the Deacon's Perspective

1. Your relationship to God determines your effectiveness as a deacon.
2. Be unshakably committed to the success of your pastor and your church.
3. Develop realistic relationships:
   - Do not expect your pastor to be perfect.
   - Seek to understand your pastor's vision.
   - Develop mutual trust and confidence.

- Be open and honest in sharing your input.
- Work to develop a friendship with your pastor.
4. Maintain right roles:
    - Differences of roles, skills, and perspectives are good, even essential.
    - Fulfill—that is, fill to the fullest—the role God has given you, but do not try to take over the role of pastor if you are a deacon.

God doesn't call men to be Lone Rangers: Commit to ministry relationships!

GPS (GETTING THE PRINCIPLES SUMMARIZED)

Find answers to these questions in the chapter.

Introduction
1. What deepens the friendship between a pastor and the deacons?

The Pastor's Perspective
Counselors
2. The text lists several verses about counsel. Write out one additional verse (with its reference) about counsel. Proverbs is a good place to look.

Co-laborers
3. What are the three levels of initiative described in terms of "doing" and "reporting"?

Communication Helpers
4. What is the wrong thing to do when someone approaches a deacon with a complaint against the pastor or any other staff member? Why? What is the deacon's goal?

Close Friends
5. Why will a pastor naturally be closer to the deacons than to most other church members?

6. What is the pastor's greatest duty in regard to the deacons?

Be Faithful: To God
7. Why did the Apostle Paul keep his body "under subjection"? (1 Corinthians 9:27)

Principles Regarding Relationships
8. List the six principles given in the text regarding pastor-deacon relationships. Choose one to expand with a sentence or two of your own. Explain why it is particularly important in your view, provide an example, or give scriptural support for the idea, or provide practical limitations and boundaries.

Principles Regarding Roles
9. What two things are in "dynamic balance"?

 APPles (Applying the Principles Practically)

Apply these ideas to your church. Discussion will often go beyond just the facts in the reading.

Introduction
1. The text describes the two extremes of pastor-deacon relationships as adversarial and cooperative. Explain briefly two or three things that you would expect to see in a cooperative relationship. This is an answer to find more in your own perspectives and ideals, not so much an answer to find in the text.

Close Friends
2. Discuss the role of the chairman of the deacons.

Be Faithful: To Your Pastor
3. Choose one of the seven "be sensitive" areas to expand on. Either take the role of pastor, expressing what you would

value; or take the role of deacon, expressing what you could do. Feel free to go beyond the specific examples of things to do given in the text. (1) Tell specific things a deacon can do to be faithful to his pastor. (2) List some possible effects of such faithfulness.

THE CONGREGATION, WORKING IN UNITY

But the manifestation of the Spirit is given to every man to profit withal. . . . For as the body is one, and hath many members, and all the members of that one body, being many, are one body: so also is Christ.
I Corinthians 12:7, 12

Anyone who comprehends the New Testament understands that the church is not a building but a gathering of people. More specifically, a local church is a gathering of born-again people who have been obedient in baptism and have joined together for worship, service, and fellowship. Just as every one of those born-again people has been indwelt by the Holy Spirit (John 14:17; Romans 8:9), every one of them is enabled by the Holy Spirit to take part in the ministry of a local church (I Corinthians 12:4-12). Unless that Spirit-enabling is allowed to work, so to speak, the local church will not function properly. Put simply, believers have work to do.

Before proceeding, however, I want to explore the statement that believers do, in fact, have work to do. The Bible teaches emphatically that good works do not produce salvation (Ephesians 2:8-9; Titus 3:5), but the Bible is equally clear that salvation does produce good works. Good works are not merely a happy by-product of salvation, but one of the very purposes for which God saved us. We are fond of quoting Ephesians 2:8-9, "By grace are ye saved . . . not of works," but the very next verse says that we have been saved to be "his workmanship, created in Christ Jesus unto good works, which God hath before ordained that we should walk in them." The book of Titus exhibits the same balanced teaching. Chapter 3 verse 5 says, "Not by works of righteousness which we have done, but according to his mercy he saved us." Just six verses earlier, however, Paul said that Jesus "gave himself for us, that he might redeem us from all iniquity, and purify unto himself *a peculiar people, zealous of good works*" (2:14). As James put it, "Faith without works is dead" (2:26). Yes, believers have work to do.

Let us consider another evidence that every believer ought to be involved in the Lord's work. The description of *pastoral* ministry found in Ephesians 4:11–12 says something very significant about the ministry of the *congregation*: "And he gave some . . . pastors and teachers; for the perfecting of the saints, for the work of the ministry." Notice that the pastor-teacher's main ministry is equipping laymen to minister! Nowhere does the New Testament paint a picture of ministry as the sole domain of pastors and deacons. Nowhere does it portray laymen merely as spectators. Pastors and deacons must realize that the more they recruit and equip church members to do the work of the Lord, the more will be accomplished for God's glory. Granted, the goal of involving 100 percent of a church's membership has probably never been accomplished in any church of more than a few members. I do think, however, that every church is capable of surpassing the usual statistic: 10 percent of the people doing 90 percent of the work.

A TRUE-LIFE EXAMPLE: YET ANOTHER MINISTRY?

Like every pastor I know, I have plenty going on. Then, on top of it all, my friend Mark walked in one day with a burden on his heart. He thought our local church needed to launch out into a whole new area of ministry. If the work of the ministry is never done— with just the projects and programs we already had—how could I smile with perfect confidence when Mark walked in with his proposal of another set of needs to meet?

GOD WORKS THROUGH THE CONGREGATION

In the local church there are two main areas of work in which the congregation must be involved. First, every believer should be a witness for the Lord Jesus Christ, evangelizing the lost. Jesus, after He was resurrected and before He left earth, commissioned His disciples to evangelize others (Matthew 28:19-20, Mark 16:15, Acts 1:8). However, it is not enough just to see people saved, God also wants to see the new believer "grow in grace and in the knowledge of our Lord and Saviour Jesus Christ" (II Peter 3:18). Matthew 28:19-20, which commands us to evangelize, also commands us to go and make disciples of all nations. The Great Commission requires both evangelism and edification.

The Work of Evangelism

Church members will play different roles in evangelism, but God orchestrates the whole. The apostle Paul said in I Corinthians 6:3, "I have planted, Apollos watered, but God gave the increase." In the body of Christ everyone should witness to others of their faith in the Lord Jesus Christ, planting the gospel seed. Other Christians will come along and witness to those who have already been confronted with the gospel. Their witness is the watering of the seed. Some, as they lead a person to a saving knowledge of the Lord Jesus Christ, will have the privilege of reaping where others have sown and watered. However, a person is never saved without God doing the work in a lost person's heart—it is God who gives the increase. It is the Holy Spirit whom the Lord has sent to draw all men unto Christ (John 12:32, John 16:7-15). God is not willing that any should perish, but that all should come to repentance (II Peter 3:9). However, God has chosen that people should do the work of evangelism: "How then shall they call on Him in whom they have not believed? and how shall they believe in Him of whom they have not heard? and how shall they hear without a preacher?" (Romans 10:14). It is the responsibility of every born-again member of the local church to be a witness of Jesus Christ to the lost world.

Effective witnessing is the sharing of the gospel of the Lord Jesus Christ in the power of the Holy Spirit, praying and leaving the results to God. Too many have put undue pressure on unbelievers to get them to pray a prayer—pressure that can result in a false profession. Titus 1:16 warns of the result: "They profess that they know God; but in works they deny him, being abominable, and disobedient, and unto every good work reprobate." We do want to persuade men (II Corinthians 5:11). Persuasion must be done through the Scriptures and the power of the Holy Spirit, not through our personality or salesmanship. I have learned that the hardest people to reach for Jesus Christ are the people who have prayed a prayer but who have not become a new creature in Christ (II Corinthians 5:17). Jesus said, "Wherefore by their fruits ye shall know them" (Matthew 7:20). As the local church evangelizes the lost, some will plant, some will water, but only God can give the increase. We must never forget our dependence on God.

It is good for a local church to have an organized visitation program for the people of the congregation. However, a formal program should not be necessary to get Christians to witness. Every member of the church encounters lost people every day. Some are our neighbors; others we work with; some we come in contact with in shopping or through recreational activities. Too many times church members may participate in an organized evangelistic effort but never personally share their faith. Both methods are important; however, if I had to have one or the other, I would prefer personal evangelism over corporate evangelism. If every person in the local church would regularly distribute tracts, invite people to church, and give a personal witness of how Christ saved him or her, many more people would be reached with the gospel of Jesus Christ and be saved (Ephesians 2:8-9). What we need in our churches are people who are soul conscious at all times and in all places.

In Acts 1:8 there is a little four-letter word, "both." It looks as though there are four different areas we are to witness in, but "both" usually refers to two. This is because of the responsibilities we have to be witnesses "both" at home and abroad—in countries all over the world through foreign missions. In the passage we are told to be witnesses both locally—in our community, in our state, in our country—and "unto the uttermost part of the earth." It is the work of local church members not only to witness personally to people in their local communities but also to give so that missionaries can be sent to the uttermost part of the earth. "And how shall they preach except they be sent?" (Romans 10:15) I believe every member of a local church not only should give 10 percent (a tithe) of his or her gross income to the general fund of a local church, but should also give over and above the tithe to worldwide evangelism. I believe that every believer has the responsibility to go to the foreign mission field with the gospel or to give so that others can go. Jesus told us, "Go ye into all the world and preach the gospel to every creature" (Mark 16:15). Not only should we be actively proclaiming the gospel to the people across the street, but we should also be proclaiming the gospel to the people across the sea. This is the work of the local church congregation.

The Work of Edification

In Ephesians 4:12 God says that the leadership of the local church is given for the "perfecting of the saints, for the work of the ministry, for the edifying of the body of Christ." It is not enough for people to be saved; God wants them to grow to be like His Son the Lord Jesus Christ (Romans 8:29, Ephesians 4:13). This is what is sometimes called the edification work in the local church. Others use the term "sanctification" (John 17:17). Just as a new baby must learn how to walk and talk in physical growth, a new born-again Christian must learn how to think like Christ (Philippians 2:5), to walk like Christ (I John 2:6), and to become like Christ (Ephesians 4:13). For this to happen, Christian brethren must love one another (John 13:35), must encourage one another (Hebrews 10:25), must bear one another's burdens (Galatians 6:2), and must teach one another (II Timothy 2:2) by word and by example (I Timothy 4:11-12).

In the local church there are several important ministries of edification that depend on congregational leadership. The Sunday school program has been a great teaching center for generations. Classes are offered for all ages in most local churches. It takes many workers from the congregation to staff an effective Sunday school program. Some need to teach the Word of God in front of the class, while others need to help in fellowship activities in and outside of class. Personal-discipleship programs are very effective in bringing the new babe to spiritual maturity. Small-group Bible studies held in homes or at the church have been very effective as Christians sharpen each other's Bible knowledge and skills (Proverbs 27:17). In order to have an effective teaching ministry within a local church, many within the congregation must get involved. Classes may be structured by age: some will teach children; some will teach teenagers; and some will teach adults. An alternative, especially for adults, is to offer classes on various topics: some will teach about the family; some will teach about Bible doctrine; some will teach about Christian living. Individual books of the Bible and many other subjects may also be addressed. No matter what is taught, and no matter to whom it is taught, edification ministries in the local church are important and require many participants.

One ministry of the local church that is extremely important is the music program. In Colossians 3:16 we read, "Let the word of Christ dwell in you richly in all wisdom, teaching and admonishing one another in psalms and hymns and spiritual songs, singing with grace in your hearts to the Lord." Music has a very powerful influence on people's lives. We are told time and time again in the Psalms to "sing unto the Lord" (Psalm 30:4; 33:2; 59:17; 71:22-23; 95:1; 96:1-2; 98:1-5; 104:33; 144:9; 149:1). The psalmist tells us, "He brought me up also out of an horrible pit, out of the miry clay and set my feet upon a rock and established my goings and He hath put a new song in my mouth, even praise unto our God. Many shall see it and fear and shall trust in the Lord" (Psalm 40:2-3). It is obvious from this passage and many others that music has a very important part both in the edifying of the saints and in the evangelizing of the lost.

Some are teaching that music is amoral and that it does not matter what kind of music we use in our local churches. I strongly disagree. Colossians 3:16 says we should sing "spiritual songs." This verse alone makes it plain that there are songs that are spiritual and songs that are not spiritual. In I Corinthians 2:15 the Bible tells us that "he that is spiritual judgeth all things." This judging must include discerning between Christ-honoring music and worldly music that dishonors the Lord (Romans 12:2, I John 2:15). Churches may or may not agree on what is spiritual and what is worldly music. However, one thing we must agree on is that there is a right and wrong in music, or surely the wrong kind of music will infiltrate the church.

We are more likely to have the right kind of music in our churches if we have the right motives for the music. Members of a local church should participate in the congregational singing enthusiastically, letting it be a real part of their worship, remembering to Whom they sing. Those who participate in special music in the choir as vocalists or as instrumentalists should minister rather than entertain. The ministry of music in the local church should speak to the spirit and not to the flesh. Those who minister in solos or small groups should not seek to draw attention to themselves, but rather should point people to Jesus Christ. Never should music be performed so that an individual or group can receive glory. Rather, music should always be presented to bring glory to God (I Corinthians 10:31). How wonderful it is to see local church members, filled with the Holy Spirit, ministering through the playing and singing of Christ-honoring music! (Ephesians 5:18-19)

GOD LEADS THROUGH THE CONGREGATION

Congregational Initiative

Several years ago Mark, one of our members, walked into my office and said, "Pastor, we need a ministry to the disabled at our church." This was a natural request for him; he and his wife have a lovely, precious, but severely disabled daughter. Mark knew what my response would be. If God burdens a person for a ministry, God is very likely calling that person to lead that ministry. And Mark was ready. He already had in his hand a typed proposal for how that ministry would work, starting with a Sunday school class helping our non-disabled members know how to reach out to the disabled. And he was prepared to teach that class.

Let God lead and work in and through His people.

Pastors and deacons should welcome initiatives from the congregation. They cannot know how God is working in each member. They do not know how each member is gifted and called to serve. Often, a new ministry will come out of a church member's unique blessings or trials or gifts or opportunities.

It is also true that you may not have a ministry because it is not God's plan for your people at a certain time. I believe in the bus ministry with all my heart and for all the right reasons. Of course, children and teens whose parents do not take them to church need someone to reach out to them. Just as much, though, our church members need the bus ministry. We can get complacent in our "holy huddle." Our people need to be reminded of the great needs all around them. If a "bus kid" is disorderly in Sunday school or writes obscenities on the bathroom walls, that is just part of the ministry, and we have plenty of adults in leadership positions and raising godly families who were once "bus kids" themselves to show what can come from the efforts of enduring, self-sacrificing bus workers. However, if there were not people willing to be bus workers, that might mean it is not God's ministry for that time. I would preach and pray, encourage and recruit. However, if the people are not burdened for the ministry, I would just keep it before the Lord and wait for His timing.

The bottom line is this: let God lead and work in and through His people. Do not be intimidated when someone comes up with an idea. You, as leaders, do not have to originate everything. You often serve better as the administrators, cheerleaders, and supporters of the ministries that God is implementing through the people of your church. Also, do not think that every time someone comes up with an idea you have to be the one to do it. The pastor, especially, must be careful here. He is not the "hired gun" to go out and take on every new thing. His role may be to help people discern whether ideas are good and workable and then to guide them as they bring to fruition the ministries God places on their hearts.

Congregational Voting

One corporate responsibility of church members is discerning God's will for the church and making it known through a vote. The pastor alone should not presume to know God's will for every decision, and even the pastor and deacons together do not always know the right thing to do. This is one reason that I believe congregational polity, or form of government, is best. If we really believe that the Spirit is at work in the heart of every believer (and not only in the hearts of "professional clergy"), congregational voting is the logical course for making major decisions. None of us can claim that we always know the mind of Christ perfectly, so it only makes sense that major decisions should be made by many people, rather than by a few. Decisions can be made with a high degree of confidence when they are made with a high degree of consensus, or agreement. For the same reason, even when a motion passes, it may be unwise to proceed when there is a significant dissenting minority.

A congregational vote is obviously a matter of the utmost importance, and it is imperative that its integrity be guarded. One simple way to ensure the integrity of a vote is to use secret ballots. Some pastors intimidate their congregation, whether they mean to or not, by asking members to raise their hands or to stand to vote yes or no. Publicly saying no when the pastor seems to want a yes vote requires courage. Because secret ballots eliminate the intimidation factor, they are a far better procedure, encouraging people to vote as they believe the Spirit is leading them. Voting by ballot is good for the leaders of the church, as well, because they need to know the true mind of the congregation.

Constitutional delegation

A written constitution is an excellent tool for maximizing the effectiveness of a congregation's decision-making process, and I believe every church ought to have one. A constitution is not required by Scripture, but it is a practical way to apply the principle that everything should be done "decently and in order" (I Corinthians 14:40). A constitution can minimize confusion by spelling out how the church will be led, how decisions will be brought to a vote, how personnel will be hired, and how finances will be managed. A doctrinal statement should be included in the constitution as well.

A constitution can also maximize the efficiency of the decision-making process. It can streamline business meetings by delegating certain responsibilities in advance. Most constitutions, for example, require a vote of the congregation for buying or selling properties, but they allow smaller money matters to be decided by the deacons. The constitution may describe by dollar limits which expenditures may be made by the pastor on his own, which require the approval of the deacons, and which must come before the church. This kind of delegation-in-advance safeguards the congregation's legitimate role without requiring a vote every time the membership needs to delegate details.

A church's constitution should be drafted by the pastor and deacons and presented to the congregation. A period of time is allowed for people to study it, and a question-and-answer session is held. There may then be a need to incorporate ideas brought out of peoples' questions. A modified version of the constitution may then be presented for review. The membership can then vote on the adoption of the constitution. The constitution can be amended as necessary in days to come. In this way, a framework is provided which will serve to facilitate the congregation's work.

GOD BLESSES UNITY IN THE CHURCH

If God works in and through individual members of the congregation to do His work, should we then not have an ordained clergy, as some denominations, or should there be no designated group of men called deacons? No, these offices are clearly called for in Scripture, and their duties are discussed at length. The point of all this is that, as these called men serve and lead, they help to create a unity among the members of a local congregation.

Leadership in One Accord

Any organization that runs smoothly depends upon the attitudes and commitment of its leadership. Being in one accord will require commitment on your part. I challenge you to commit to unity. There are many examples of unity in God's Word. Let us begin where the church began: the early chapters of Acts.

> *And when they were come in, they went up into an upper room, where abode both Peter, and James, and John, and Andrew, Philip, and Thomas, Bartholomew, and Matthew, James the son of Alphaeus, and Simon Zelotes, and Judas the brother of James. These all continued with one accord in prayer and supplication, with the women, and Mary the mother of Jesus, and with his brethren.*
> Acts 1:13-14

As the church age was being ushered in, we find the apostles setting the example of unity. Having just come through the worst of times and the best of times, they were together in one place and "with one accord," or in agreement.

The apostles' focus was on prayer. In order for us as deacons and pastors to be in unity and to be of one accord, we must have the mind of Christ. This only comes through prayer. If you really want to fall in love with your pastor or fellow deacons, try praying for them. Praying for someone stifles bitterness and brings love.

Our monthly deacons meetings always begin with a time of prayer and devotions. Each month a different deacon presents a devotional Bible study, and all of us pray together. Often this time lasts for an hour or more. Sound dull? Not at all! You need to see the excitement of a group of men committed to each other and to the work of God. This time is the life blood of unity and is a key to the strength of the church.

Christians in One Accord

As Christians develop right relationships with each other, God will be pleased. In the early church, as Christians were filled with the Holy

Spirit and approximately three thousand people were saved on the day of Pentecost, unity was one mark of that large group:

> *And they continued stedfastly in the apostles' doctrine and fellowship, and in breaking of bread, and in prayers. . . . And they, continuing daily with one accord in the temple, and breaking bread from house to house, did eat their meat with gladness and singleness of heart, Praising God, and having favour with all the people. And the Lord added to the church daily such as should be saved.*
> Acts 2:42, 46-47

When persecution came, the unity was only increased. After James and John were interrogated and threatened by the same leaders who had crucified the Lord, they reported back to the church.

> *And being let go, they went to their own company, and reported all that the chief priest and elders had said unto them. And when they heard that, they lifted up their voice to God <u>with one accord</u>, and said, Lord, thou art God, which hast made heaven, and earth, and the sea, and all that in them is.*
> Acts 4:23-24

When the leadership is in one accord, the congregation can be also.

Results of Being in One Accord

Missionaries are sent
A genuine care for the lost is present in a unified group of believers. Let us move forward to Acts chapter 8. "Therefore, they that were scattered abroad went everywhere preaching the word. Then Philip went down to the city of Samaria, and preached Christ unto them" (Acts 8:4-5).

Souls are saved
"And the people with one accord gave heed unto those things which Philip spoke, hearing and seeing the miracles which he did" (Acts 8:6).

People have joy
"And there was great joy in that city" (Acts 8:8). Unity will bring great joy to your church and to the heart of God.

In his high priestly prayer, Jesus prayed, "That they all may be one; as thou, Father, art in me, and I in thee, that they also may be one in us: that the world may believe that thou hast sent me" (John 17:21). Unity in the local church was important to Jesus. Paul the Apostle prized unity too: he exhorted the Ephesians to walk worthy of their calling, "endeavoring to keep the unity of the Spirit in the bond of peace" (Ephesians 4:1, 3). Such unity cannot be maintained unless pastors and deacons understand the proper role and work of the congregation and teach every church member to do his part.

In Ephesians 2:8-9 we are told that we are saved through faith and not of works. This is the beautiful truth of salvation through our Lord and Savior Jesus Christ. It is a gift (Romans 6:23). You cannot earn it; you cannot work for it; you cannot obtain it by your own merits. You can only receive it by believing on the Lord Jesus Christ (John 1:12). However, in Ephesians 2:10 Christians are described as God's "workmanship created in Christ Jesus unto good works." God did not save us by works, but He did save us so we would work for Him here on this earth. In Philippians 2:12 we are told to "work out your own salvation with fear and trembling." This is not teaching us that we are saved by working, but it is teaching us that once we are saved, we should be willing to work. Remember, the saints are being perfected by the leadership of the local church so they can do the "work of the ministry" (Ephesians 4:12). The strength of the local church is determined by the people in the local church. As the congregation works to reach the lost, to edify the saints, and to minister to one another, then will the body be built up and the work of our Lord Jesus Christ will be expanded, both locally and internationally.

CHAPTER REVIEW

1. We are not saved by works, but we are saved to work.
2. The work of the pastor is to prepare the congregation for ministry.
3. All ministries of the church fit into two distinct, though overlapping, categories:

- Evangelization
- Edification

4. The music of the church is extremely important. It must be the right kind of music presented with the right motives.

5. God leads through the congregation.
   - New ministries
   - Congregational voting

6. A church constitution helps the church do all things decently and in order.

7. God blesses unity in the church.

God has gifted every Christian: Value each one.

GPS (GETTING THE PRINCIPLES SUMMARIZED)

Find answers to these questions in the chapter.

Introduction
1. What definition does the text offer for "local church"?
2. What is the relationship between salvation, grace, and good works?
3. According to Ephesians 4:11-12, what is the main ministry of the pastor?

God Works through the Congregation
4. What are the two broad areas which the Great Commission requires? (Matthew 28:19-20)

The Work of Evangelism
5. How does the text define evangelism?

The Work of Edification
6. What synonyms are offered for edification?
7. What are some right and wrong motives for music in the church?

Congregational Voting
8. Why is the ballot a good way to take a church vote, rather than a show of hands?

Constitutional Delegation
9. Who draws up a constitution?

Christians in One Accord
10. What resulted from the persecution of the early church?

Results of Being in One Accord
11. Read Acts 8:4–8. List the results of a Holy Spirit-filled "congregation" acting in unity.

 APPles (Applying the Principles Practically)

Apply these ideas to your church. Discussion will often go beyond just the facts in the reading.

The Work of Evangelism
1.   The text states that the hardest people to win to Christ are those who have made a false profession of faith. What can a soulwinner do to lessen the likelihood of that happening?

The Work of Edification
2.   Discuss whether music, apart from the words, has a "right or wrong" about it (moral) or is just a matter of preference, culture, or personal taste (amoral).

Congregational Initiative
3.   Discuss the roles of the pastor and the church member in starting new ministries.

Congregational Voting
4.   Discuss the value of a congregational vote as one means of discerning the will of God for a given decision.

Leadership in One Accord
5. What promotes unity among the leaders of a local church?

Chapter 9 Carl Herbster

LET'S TALK FINANCES

If therefore ye have not been faithful in the unrighteous mammon, who will commit to your trust the true riches?
Luke 16:11

Money is not inherently evil. In fact, the Bible repeatedly instructs us in its wise use. We are commanded to invest material wealth in spiritual work so that eternal riches can be obtained. Clearly, money can be a tremendous asset for ministry. But the Bible also issues stern warnings about money. First Timothy 6:10, for example, says, "The love of money is the root of all evil." Many local churches have experienced terrible problems simply because finances were not handled wisely. Money, like fire, can be extremely useful or extremely destructive. When money is carefully managed, it is a blessing; but when it is loved and coveted, or when it is unwisely used, it becomes a curse.

Money, like fire, can be extremely useful or extremely destructive.

To bring a local church's financial practice into conformity with biblical teaching, every member should understand the basics. But it is doubly important for pastors and deacons to understand these matters thoroughly. Someone has observed that three things destroy pastors and deacons: fame, females, and finances. This need not be the case. I believe the following principles and procedures will facilitate a Christ-honoring use of money in the local church.

A TRUE-LIFE EXAMPLE: WHEN THE MONEY WASN'T THERE

We were blindsided by this one. Our Christian school, although a ministry of our church, is open to students from other churches of like faith.

That is good; not every pastor is called to lead a Christian school. But when two other Christian schools were opened in our area, the decrease in our enrollment was not seen until we were into the summer months. Every teacher we had was a skilled teacher, committed to the Lord, to our church, and to the cause of Christian education. However, it became clear as the summer went on that the tuitions were not going to be what we had budgeted for. The revised income clearly would not pay all of the teachers' salaries. What can the pastor and deacons do?

FOUNDATIONAL PRINCIPLES FOR MANAGING CHURCH FINANCES

The Principle of Stewardship

Stewardship is the fundamental principle that must govern the financial policies of a local church. Many individuals and families have been robbed of choice blessings because they did not understand faithful stewardship. Sadly, the same is true for many churches. The Psalmist says, "The earth is the Lord's, and the fulness thereof; the world, and they that dwell therein" (Psalm 24:1). The Creator's ownership is universal and absolute. So what is our role? We are not owners, but stewards, and stewards must be faithful: "Moreover it is required in stewards, that a man be found faithful" (I Corinthians 4:2).

Jesus Himself both taught and illustrated stewardship in the parable of the talents recorded in Matthew 25:14-30. This parable teaches us first that we are merely managers of someone else's money, and second that we will be held accountable. These two concepts provide the framework for every other principle and procedure we will discuss, because, ultimately, money exists to glorify its Owner. "Whether therefore ye eat, or drink, or whatsoever ye do,"—including financial management!—"do all to the glory of God" (I Corinthians 10:31).

The Principle of Purpose

The principle of stewardship tells us *what* we must do with money: use it to glorify the One who really owns it. The principle of purpose tells us *how*. I never tire of repeating that the ultimate purpose of the local church is to develop Christlikeness in believers (Matthew 28:19-20, Romans 8:29), and when a church invests its money in that purpose, God is glorified.

Any policy that keeps money from being invested in eternity should be changed immediately. Any practice that wastes money or hoards it rather than putting it to work must be terminated without delay. In the short term, money may be spent, saved, or invested. In the long term, however, every single dollar must be spent in making disciples and planting other churches that will do the same. Because we do not know tomorrow, we must keep some funds in reserve for cash flow, saving for maintenance or building projects, and so on. However, if I could have perfect knowledge of the future and knew when the Lord would return, it would be my goal to have not one dime in the bank. When Christ came, I would have it all invested in reaching people for Him!

The Principle of Being Givers, not Getters

"Be a giver, not a getter." This is the challenge church leaders frequently make to their congregations. After all, the Bible promises, "Give and it shall be given unto you" (Luke 6:38). Pastors and deacons, however, must be willing to take the same challenge themselves. We rejoice when money flows into our church funds, but how much money flows out into other ministries? Churches and church leaders ought to give generously to other ministries. This implies, first and foremost, an active missions program which is reaching the world with the gospel of Jesus Christ. Some churches even give money out of their building fund for building projects on the foreign mission field.

The principle of being givers rather than getters demands a step of faith. Pastors and deacons sometimes worry about how the needs of their ministry will be met. We must remind ourselves of Philippians 4:19: "But my God shall supply all your need according to his riches in glory by Christ Jesus." The Philippian church had given generously to other ministries, and Paul promised that God would honor that. God is a giver, and He delights in blessing givers.

The Principle of Seeking Help

Church leaders must be willing to seek the help of others. Of course, when it comes to seeking others' help, God should be number one on the list. Scripture places a strong emphasis on praying about every aspect of life, and especially for the work of the church. Specifically, we are encouraged to ask God to supply. John 14:13 says, "And whatsoever ye shall ask in my name, that will I do, that the Father may be glorified in the Son." First John 3:22 says, "And whatsoever we ask, we receive of him, because we keep his commandments, and do those things that are pleasing in his sight." God is generous in His giving; the Psalmist even described Him as One that "hath pleasure in the prosperity of his servant" (Psalm 35:27). God thrills in providing for His children, and we should continually ask Him to do so in our local churches.

God not only supplies funds, He also supplies wisdom, and sometimes He does this through people. Christian leaders, therefore, should never be afraid to utilize the expertise of others. Sometimes a church has deacons who are particularly knowledgeable about money matters, and the pastor and congregation may choose to delegate much of the financial oversight to those men. On the other hand, there are often businessmen in the church who are not deacons but do have great financial knowledge. Men who are in leadership would do well to consult those businessmen. Remember, "the way of a fool is right in his own eyes: but he that hearkeneth unto counsel is wise" (Proverbs 12:15).

In many churches, the men who oversee the finances are called trustees. However, this term is nowhere to be found in the New Testament; it is an office which has been established by state governments. In the Scriptures, only pastors and deacons are named. It is best, therefore, to appoint certain deacons to serve as a finance committee so that they can fulfill state requirements of having trustees, while the church maintains biblical polity. I would recommend referring to these men publicly as deacons or the finance committee to avoid confusing people about the offices outlined in the Bible.

BASIC PROCEDURES FOR MANAGING CHURCH FINANCES

Establish a Budget and Follow it

Amazingly, many churches operate without a budget, and some churches that *do* have budgets only established them when they started

Christian schools. Having a budget is basic. Whether large or small, a local church *must* have a budget which estimates income and expenses using the previous year's record as a basis. The budget should be approved by congregational vote and executed on a daily basis by the pastor and his staff.

Money in the budget does not necessarily mean there is money in the bank!

Establishing a budget is purely academic unless you strive to work within the budget, and, to work within the budget, you must understand the difference between budget and cash. The fact that there is money in the budget does not necessarily mean that there is money in the bank! Before authorizing expenditures, both the cash position and the budget position must be considered. The only way to generate cash for future expenditures is to spend less money than you have, so as to have an excess of funds at the end of the year. If the giving is below budget, then the spending must be below budget. If the income has been greater than budgeted, it is still advisable to keep spending within the budget in order to generate extra funds for unexpected needs. You may also find that some expenses were not as great as the budgeted amount—that can be a means of saving for the future too. The fact that there is money in the budget does not mean that it must be spent.

In most churches' bills can be paid weekly, with the checks being signed by appropriate individuals on the weekend. Cash funds can be established to cover special needs that arise during the week, but receipts should always be required for reimbursement. Pastors can use personal credit cards for transportation expenses, ministry meals, and other necessary purchases that have been approved by the church. The pastors should then be reimbursed on a monthly basis so that their credit cards can be paid off without accruing interest.

Establish Spending Limits within the Budget

Spending limits must be established within the budget. A purchase-order system should be put in place so that all expenditures have to be pre-approved. A petty cash fund can be set up to handle small, daily purchases, but it is wise to require a purchase order for any expense over one hundred dollars. In this way, everyone will be held accountable for spending. Different individuals within the organization may have higher spending limits than others because of their responsibility, but there ought to be a limit above which no one may spend money without the approval of the deacons who form the finance committee. Spending over a thousand dollars without the approval of several key leaders in the church is always unwise.

In our ministry, spending limits are determined by level of authority on the organizational chart. All personnel can spend money within their budget up to one hundred dollars without approval from their superior. Between one hundred dollars and three hundred dollars, it takes an administrator's approval for these expenditures. Anything over three hundred dollars, but less than five hundred dollars, can be approved by the executive staff. Expenditures over five hundred dollars, but less than one thousand dollars, require the approval of the senior pastor. Any purchases over one thousand dollars should be approved by the finance committee. In this way no one is making a major purchase without the approval of others.

For any church, purchase orders should go to the business office or church treasurer for final approval. It is possible to have money approved in the budget and at the same time not to have money in the bank because of a lack of giving in the ministry. The business office must not approve purchase orders for expenses if there is not money in the bank to pay the bills once they are received.

It is also possible to have money in the bank but not have money approved within the budget. Of course, this is a great position for a church to be in. However, staff members should not be allowed to overspend their budget, even if there is extra money in the bank. These funds should be saved for special projects such as new buildings, replacing equipment, or the taking on of additional missionaries. The financial secretary, business manager, or purchasing coordinator should be assigned in every local church to regularly evaluate what is in the budget and what is in the bank. All purchase orders should require the signature of this person.

Maintain Accountability

An accountability structure for everyone who handles church funds is absolutely necessary. Several simple guidelines can be put into place to prevent not only temptation but also false accusations. First, there should always be more than one person handling and counting the offerings. Second, a money deposit should be verified with a deposit slip. Third, no one should have sole check-signing authority: always require a dual signature on checks for large amounts. The two could be the pastor and the church treasurer. Even though a pastor or deacon may never do anything unethical, sole check-signing authority could give church members the wrong impression. It could also hurt the church's testimony in the community. Someone, usually the church treasurer should regularly review the check register.

In addition to individual accountability, the entire ministry team can be held accountable through financial reporting. A monthly report should be made to the deacons or finance committee, and a report should be given to the whole congregation at least quarterly. Questions about the report can be handled privately. It is usually unwise to discuss financial concerns in an open meeting, and very few people will have major concerns. Others in the congregation may have points on which they disagree with the pastor and the majority of deacons about how some financial matters should be handled. Addressing questions in a private meeting rather than in a public forum saves time and will eliminate the possibility of grandstanding or the spreading of discord among the brethren by those who want to call attention to their viewpoints.

We have done this in two ways. One is to present the annual budget at a business meeting after the Wednesday night service. We then have a question/answer time on Sunday afternoon before the vote on Sunday night. The other way is to present the matter on Wednesday night and have a question/answer session for everyone who wants to stay after the service. Either way allows people to hear the recommendation but does not require them to stay for all the discussion that might come from the question/answer time.

Another very important means of accountability is the annual audit. This should be done by an outside accounting firm contracted by the church. The fee for the audit will vary depending on the size of church and the variety of ministries under the local church. This audit will verify that the accounting procedures of the local church and the reports that have been given are consistent with acceptable practices in the financial world. It will also verify that funds reported to be in the bank are actually there. It is a good idea to do an asset audit along with the financial audit every three to five years. This will verify the value of assets reported on the balance sheet. Financial and asset audits will hold the church and its leaders accountable for reporting finances properly and will help to protect them from the temptation of stealing from the Lord and the local ministry. Sad to say, several ministries we are aware of have had individuals embezzle money through inappropriate accounting and actions. Annual audits by an agency outside of the church will help prevent this from happening. This is also a means to "provide things honest in the sight of all men" (Romans 12:17).

Handle Borrowing Wisely

Borrowing is not prohibited in the Bible, but it *is* discouraged; therefore assuming debt should be done cautiously. The governing financial principle of the Scriptures is stewardship, and paying heavy interest is not normally advantageous in managing the church's resources. The use of charge cards should be avoided, and facilities should never be mortgaged above fifty percent of the value of the church's assets. The one exception for borrowing may be a purchase of properties or the construction of facilities which escalate in value. Construction costs go up every year, and the wise borrowing of funds to purchase property or construct facilities may actually save the church money in the long run. In any case, the church should not be committed to a loan without a congregational vote.

The goal of every church should be to lower debt so as to pay as little interest as possible. Therefore, the restructuring of loans should be something church leadership evaluates on an annual basis. Thousands of dollars can be saved by investigating the lending practices of various banks. As loans are paid down, banks often will give lower interest rates because of the lack of risk in making the loan. It should not be necessary for a church to vote on the restructuring of its debt. The finance committee or deacons should be able to do this as a part of their regular responsibilities for the church. However, never should the debt of a church be increased without a vote from the congregation.

SOME PROBLEMS IN MANAGING CHURCH FINANCES

Lack of Income

The number one problem within local church ministries is insufficient income to do all the ministry the church would like to do. This problem is created because of a lack of giving by the church membership. There are few churches in our country in which more than 50 percent of the congregation tithes to the local church. Therefore, there are a number of people who are "robbing God" (Malachi 3:6-7). God has always challenged His people to bring the tithes into the storehouse. This is both Old Testament and New Testament teaching. Jesus, in Matthew 23:23, verified the importance of tithing. However, this is not a maximum but a minimum. In the New Testament we should give as the Lord has prospered us (I Corinthians 16:2). If all the people in our local churches would tithe and would give over the tithe as the Lord has prospered them, we would have plenty of resources to do the work of the Lord.

Giving is not a subject most pastors like to preach on. However, it is necessary to deal with this topic on a regular basis. Many churches like to have a stewardship month once a year. Some include their missions conference along with this special stewardship emphasis. Whether the church has a stewardship month or not, giving should be proclaimed regularly from the pulpits of our local churches.

It would also be wise for churches to have a Sunday school class on financial management. Many times people are not giving to their local church properly because they are not handling their individual finances effectively. A financial management class offered in Sunday school could help people understand how they could better handle their finances and thereby help them make giving to the local church the priority that God wants it to be. Proverbs 3:9-10 is not a trick by which we can twist God's arm, but it is a statement of the general course of God's working: "Honour the Lord with thy substance, and with the firstfruits of all thine increase: So shall thy barns be filled with plenty, and thy presses shall burst out with new wine."

Individual counseling should be provided for those who want personal help and personal accountability. People learn that the joy of giving will not only help the local church expand the ministry, but will also bring to themselves many blessings from the Lord (Malachi 3:8, Luke 16:11). These blessings are not always financial. Luke 16:11 speaks of the "true riches" as in contrast to "the unrighteous mammon" (money), implying that other blessings, such as peace, direction, and purpose, are of greater value.

Misplaced Spending Priorities

As we have seen before, people should take priority over properties. However, church finances that should be spent on personnel are often spent on buildings. I have said many times to people in our church, "Show me your checkbook, and I'll show you your priorities." What is good for our people is also good for us as leaders of local churches. Show me the spending of a local church ministry, and I will show you what is most important to them. There is no question about what is most important to God—people. Therefore, we should take care of the needs of our people, even if we have to put up with less than we desire in our facilities.

This became very practical to me one year when we lost one hundred students from our Christian school. Two new Christian schools opened in our area. We did not see the effect of that change until we were into the summer months. We were in the middle of a building campaign, as well. Without the proper student population and with the increased building costs, it would have been easy to lay off staff to balance the budget. To make these layoffs during the last months before the new school year would have put the affected teachers in dire straits. However, our deacons showed their priority on people by their willingness to fund the Christian school staff through the church budget so that no layoffs were necessary. The decision was made to cut other costs so that all the personnel could stay in the ministry and not have to relocate their families at the last moment. The priority on people was clearly demonstrated to our church through this decision.

It does not always work out that way. When the income shortfall is long-term, and the overall budget cannot continue to absorb the change, it may be necessary to reduce the size of the staff. If this is done, it should be done with as much warning as possible. There may be staff members who were considering a change anyway, and knowing of the impending need for downsizing may clarify God's leadership for them. If the church leadership must make these difficult decisions, it should be done with utmost consideration for the people involved. It may be that the pastor or others can help people make the contacts they need for continuing their ministry or employment elsewhere.

Sometimes monies are spent on frills that really do not help the ministry of the local church. Our buildings should look nice, but they do not need to be extravagant, looking more like high-class hotels than efficient local church ministries. Staff should be paid well, but never should be paid at the level of income they could be making in the secular world. It would be dangerous for people to enter full-time Christian work because it pays well—dangerous for the ministry and for the people themselves. High tech equipment is nice, but not necessary, if we are limiting our missions outreach because of our technological expenditures. Local church leadership should evaluate the priorities in ministry and make sure that their expenditures through the local church match these priorities.

Honorariums

Most local churches will have guest speakers on a regular basis. These may be evangelists, missionaries, college personnel, or even visiting pastors from other local churches. Some churches have established a normal honorarium they give to these special speakers. This is a mistake. I believe there should be a minimal amount a church gives an outside speaker for filling the pulpit. However, I do not believe there should be a maximum amount. The best way to handle outside speakers is to allow the people to give to that speaker or his ministry as they are led of the Lord. Take up the usual offering for the needs of the church at the usual time. Then a second offering should be taken after the speaker has finished, and everything that comes in should be passed on to the guest speaker. If the amount given is not at least the minimum that the church has established, the difference can be added from the budget. However, most of the time, special offerings will be much more than the minimum honorariums established by most churches. This will not only properly meet the needs of the special guests but will also save money in the honorarium budget of the local church.

There are two main reasons for using these special offerings rather than honorariums. First, it encourages the people to give to the ministries of others. Some will be burdened for certain speakers more than others will. Giving allows individual church members the opportunity to feel a part of the ministry that the special speaker had in their local church and in the speaker's ministry elsewhere. People receive the blessing when they give to the servant of the Lord. "Give, and it shall be given unto you" (Luke 6:38). The other reason for taking special offerings is to manage the budget more effectively. A "special offerings income and expense account" can be established. This is a flow-through account. *Flow-through* means that everything that comes in as income will also go out as expenses. By having a special offering account, a local church is not limited on the number of speakers they can have within a given budget year. If only honorariums are budgeted, once the honorarium budget is depleted, the local church is limited on the use of outside speakers. I believe it is important for every church to have the flexibility to use guest preachers when they are needed, no matter what the financial cost. Special offerings allow this flexibility to the local church.

Of course I believe expenses (lodging, meals, perhaps travel) for outside speakers could be covered through the budget. If people are told they are giving to the *love offering* of the evangelist, then it should be a gift over and above expenses. If the people are told the offering is to pay the speakers expenses and to give him a special gift from the church, then leadership should make sure the offering is not used for expenses only. God's people will never go wrong taking care of God's servants.

People Handling Finances Who Do Not Understand Finances

The Bible is clear in Luke that sometimes people in this world are wiser about finances than the children of light (16:8). Not only should a pastor be well-schooled in personal and ministry finances, but also those who serve on the finance committee should possess a thorough understanding of finances and of the budgeting and spending processes. Thank the Lord, in most local churches there are people who handle finances every day in their businesses. These people can assist in budget matters. However, leadership of the local church should make sure that those who are responsible for the accounting and spending of the Lord's money are well acquainted with proper financial policies and procedures.

In our local church the finance committee is appointed by the chairman of the deacons with the approval of the pastor. They are not called trustees even though the constitution states that "the finance committee will serve as the trustees of the church as required by the state." The finance committee, therefore, is made up of deacons who are fulfilling the requirement of the state to have trustees over the local church ministry as a not-for-profit corporation. I would strongly discourage churches from having "trustees" that do not qualify as deacons. I would also discourage churches from calling these men "trustees" since this can greatly confuse Christians about the biblical requirement for this office, which is entrusted to deacons. The finance committee can fulfill the role of trustees without taking the title.

No matter what a church decides to call those responsible for the finances of the local church, these men ought to remember that they are accountable to God and the membership of the local congregation. They should constantly be improving their skills in the area of finances through reading, through seminars, and even through taking classes on finances. It is very helpful if at least one of the finance committee members is an accountant or has accounting experience. In order to manage the church finances properly, local bodies of believers need to have on their finance committees men who are well schooled in financial management. There is no assurance, however, that a prosperous person will be a good deacon or even a good manager of church funds. Avoid the trap of nominating someone to be a deacon just because he is a successful businessman. However, if men have done a good job with their personal finances, and they are otherwise qualified as deacons, it is a good sign they will do well with the church finances also.

Much more could be said about finances, but these basic principles and policies are a good starting place for establishing sound financial practice. They will make a church financially strong as well as keeping it financially accountable. The pastor, deacons, and church members must understand proper procedures and must have mutual accountability and trust. The ultimate accountability, of course, is the account we will give one day to God. Our desire should be to hear the same commendation as the wise servants in the parable of the talents: "Well done, thou good and faithful servant: thou hast been faithful over a few things, I will make thee ruler over many things: enter thou into the joy of thy lord" (Matthew 25:21).

CHAPTER REVIEW

1. Biblical principles of finance:
    *   Stewardship: God owns it all.
    *   Purpose: Church finances should glorify God.

- Giving: The church should seek to give to the greater work of Christ.
- Help: We are commanded to seek counsel.
  - First, pray about everything—income, expenses, and wisdom in management.
  - Second, seek the help of people to whom God has given financial wisdom.
2. Wise procedures of finance:
  - Establish a budget and follow it!
  - Establish spending limits—how much money requires what level of approval.
  - Maintain accountability—trust and verify.
  - A congregational vote is needed for borrowing or increasing debt.
3. Proactive anticipation of common dangers:
  - Lack of income.
  - Unwise spending.
  - Honorariums instead of offerings.
  - Unskilled financial managers.

Money is a tool of service: Use this tool skillfully!

 ## GPS (GETTING THE PRINCIPLES SUMMARIZED)

Find answers to these questions in the chapter.

Introduction
1. How is money like fire?

The Principle of Stewardship
2. What is the "fundamental principle" of church finances? Why?
3. What are the two principles found in the parable of the talents, Matthew 25:14–30?

The Principle of Purpose
4. How is God glorified in the use of money?

The Principle of Being Givers
5. Give examples of ways a church gives.

The Principle of Seeking Help
6. To whom can the pastors and deacons look for financial wisdom?

Establish a Budget
7. List one or two principles which stand out to you in this section.

Establish Spending Limits within the Budget
8. What are the petty cash, $100, and $1000 suggested guidelines?

Maintain Accountability
9. Why do churches need to have a structured system of accountability.
10. List six guidelines that can prevent temptation and false accusation.

Lack of Income
11. What is the connection between finances and spiritual fruit?

Misplaced Spending Priorities
12. How does our budget reflect our priorities?

People Handling Finances Who Do Not Understand Finances
13. What two areas must a deacon be skilled in if he is to serve on the finance committee?

 APPles (Applying the Principles Practically)

Apply these ideas to your church. Discussion will often go beyond just the facts in the reading.

The Principle of Stewardship
1. What are some possible contrasts to stewardship? That is, how do people go wrong on this?

The Principle of Purpose
2. How can one balance using money to get ministry done now and preparing for the future.

Establish a Budget and Follow It
3. Is a budget restrictive?

Maintain Accountability
4. Why should a church have audits?

Lack of Income
5. Should a pastor preach about money?

Honorariums
6. How are offerings for honorariums better than a budgeted amount?

DEALING WITH DIFFICULTIES

In the world ye shall have tribulation: but be of good cheer; I have overcome the world.
John 16:33

Every church has problems that must be dealt with. Jesus said in John 16:33, "In the world ye shall have tribulation." This is definitely true in our society as a whole, and, yes, even in our local churches. When you are dealing with people, you know you will be dealing with their problems: the more people, the more problems. However, Jesus also said in that same verse, "Be of good cheer; I have overcome the world." By dealing with problems biblically, we can overcome them and even grow through them.

A TRUE-LIFE EXAMPLE: WHEN YOUR IN-BOX READS LIKE JOB CHAPTER 1

You remember the first chapter of Job: with divine permission, Satan orchestrated a series of disaster reports characterized by "while he was yet speaking, there came also another. . . ." I am no Job, but there came a year in my ministry when the church was hit with one devastating problem after another. Satan had gotten a number of footholds, all the way from a staff member being unfaithful to his wife to a bitter church member actively campaigning to get me to leave. It seemed that I was always bringing some matter to the deacons and then before the church. What can keep a pastor and the deacons able to minister at such a time? How do you comfort, lead, and protect the congregation? What do you do when the bottom drops out?

THE PROPER PERSPECTIVE FOR UNDERSTANDING DIFFICULTIES

"When the enemy comes in like a flood"

Within a ministry, there are normal difficulties that pastors and deacons must handle, and there are also times when extraordinary difficulties enter a local church ministry. Normal situations include marriage problems, challenges with children, financial difficulties, problems with the tongue, physical difficulties, and loss of loved ones. Any pastor will deal with this type of problem on a regular basis. He must always be available in time of need and will allow the deacons to help with some of these situations to the extent that they are able and available.

Extraordinary difficulties are ones that may or may not happen within the life of a church or pastor. However, pastors and deacons must always be ready to deal with the extraordinary when it comes their way. In nineteen years of ministry, I had never dealt with even one of the five challenges that came my way in the twentieth year. That year started with a slanderous letter about me and the ministry being sent not only to our church membership but also to leaders in the Christian school movement across the country. We also had an individual report our church to the Missouri Secretary of State's office, accusing us of running a bank. Because of that accusation an uncomplimentary newspaper article was written about the church in the *Kansas City Star*. The year started out with extraordinary difficulties, but the worst was yet to come.

In June of that year, shortly after I had returned from a missions trip, the associate pastor informed me of a conversation he had had with an individual accusing our youth pastor of immorality. In my years at the church, we had never faced unfaithfulness in a pastoral staff member. The youth pastor was confronted, and he confessed, both privately and publicly. He resigned his position and worked at reconciling his marriage. Praise the Lord, he is together with his wife today, although they have moved to another state, and he is no longer serving as a pastor.

Soon after this tragic event, an auditor whom we had hired to review our books informed me and the finance committee about a possible embezzlement having been done by our former business manager.

The auditor confronted the individual, and he confessed to the auditor, to me, and to our finance committee. He did not realize how much he had stolen from the ministry during a seven year period—over a million dollars. We had to report it to the police, since it was a criminal matter extending beyond our ministry, and they followed through on the prosecution.[3] It was impossible to recover all the funds that were taken; however, we learned not just to trust but also to verify.

God was exposing sin and I was dealing with situations before the church on Wednesday nights almost weekly. I preached a message on Numbers 32:23: "Be sure your sin will find you out." I encouraged everyone in our church to get sin out before God had to expose it publicly. With renewed passion, I presented the truth of Proverbs 28:13: "He that covereth his sins shall not prosper, but whosoever confesseth and forsaketh them shall have mercy." Little did I know there was a sin still being covered, a sin that God would bring to light.

A police officer who is a member of our ministry informed me that one of our deacons was having inappropriate email contact with some of our young people. She also had discovered that he had proceeded beyond email and had done some inappropriate things in the presence of young people. Still, we did not know the extent of his wrongdoing until he was charged by two families with child molestation. Before the police contacted this deacon, I confronted him with his sin. At first he denied the charges but resigned his position as deacon. Soon, however, he confessed to inappropriate actions with young people and surrendered himself to the police department. As you can imagine, all the news media of Kansas City covered this tragic situation, and we had to deal with reporters from the press, radio, and TV for several weeks. The former deacon was charged and convicted of child molestation and was sent to jail.

Because of all these situations, people were leaving our church, and some were calling for my resignation as pastor. Of course I had to evaluate prayerfully what God was teaching me and what He wanted me to do in the days ahead. The deacons were wonderful counselors and

---

3 The Scripture is clear that we should not take a brother to court to settle our disputes (I Corinthians 6). But the Scripture is also clear that "He that covereth his sins shall not prosper" (Proverbs 28:13). I can forgive an offense against myself, and the church can vote to forgive an offense against the church; but these crimes reached across state lines, broke state and federal laws, and involved people and organizations outside of our local church. To do anything but report it to the authorities would have been to join with the former business manager in covering his sin.

great encouragers to me during this time. They had to meet with several disgruntled church members and hear their complaints about me and the ministry. They listened carefully, evaluated thoroughly. Through it all, they found nothing in which I was at fault, and they supported me completely. We had many long meetings discussing what was taking place in our ministry and many wonderful prayer times asking God to give us wisdom and to bring His people through. Thank the Lord, He directed our steps and protected His work and His people.

"The Spirit of the Lord shall lift up a standard"

During this time, I started preaching a series of messages from the book of James. In the very first chapter God gives some wonderful instruction on how to deal with difficulties. God's Word teaches in James 1:2, "My brethren, count it all joy when you fall into divers temptations." We do not rejoice in the problem, but we can rejoice in the providence of God. "All things work together for good to them that love God, to them who are the called according to His purpose" (Romans 8:28). We are admonished in Philippians 4:4, "Rejoice in the Lord alway, and again I say rejoice." We cannot always rejoice in the situation, but we can rejoice in the fact that God is still in control. In I Peter 4:12, the Bible says, "Beloved, think it not strange concerning the fiery trial which is to try you, as though some strange thing happened unto you, but rejoice inasmuch as ye are partakers of Christ's sufferings; that, when his glory shall be revealed, ye may be glad also with exceeding joy." If we suffer for righteousness sake, we are suffering even as Christ suffered. Jesus Himself said, "Blessed are ye, when men shall revile you, and persecute you, and shall say all manner of evil against you falsely, for my sake. Rejoice, and be exceeding glad: for great is your reward in Heaven: for so persecuted they the prophets who were before you" (Matthew 5:11-12). We do not always know the reason for the trial, but we can rejoice in the fact that God has a perfect plan for our lives. In dealing with difficulties, our first great lesson is to *rejoice in the providence of God.*

> *We cannot always rejoice in the situation, but we can rejoice in the fact that God is still in control.*

The second thing we learn from James 1 about dealing with difficulties is to *remember the purpose of God:* "Knowing this, that the trying of your faith worketh patience. But let patience have her perfect work, that ye may be perfect and entire, wanting nothing" (James 1:3-4). God's eternal purpose is that we would be conformed to the image of His Son, Jesus Christ (Romans 8:29). We are told in Philippians 2:5 to "let this mind be in you, which was also in Christ Jesus." God is trying to mature us through the pressures of life. He is trying to teach us to respond to difficulties the way Jesus responded, "who, when he was reviled, reviled not again; when he suffered, he threatened not; but committed himself to Him that judgeth righteously" (I Peter 2:23). Even when He was crucified unjustifiably, He called out from the cross, "Father, forgive them; for they know not what they do" (Luke 23:34). The Bible also instructs us to "be not overcome of evil, but overcome evil with good" (Romans 12:21), and "let us do good unto all men, especially unto them who are of the household of faith" (Galatians 6:10). Of course, Job suffered many trials, and he said, "He knoweth the way that I take: when he hath tried me, I shall come forth as gold" (Job 23:10). Just like a weightlifter has to put on more weights to strengthen his muscles, God has to bring difficult situations into our lives to strengthen our trust in Him (Proverbs 3:5-6). God wants to make us into the image of Jesus Christ. Therefore, we must suffer some trials, even as Christ suffered, so that we can fulfill the purpose of God, Christlikeness.

Not only does James teach us that we must rejoice in the providence of God and remember the purpose of God, but in verse 5, he urges us to *rely on the promise from God*. "If any of you lack wisdom, let him ask of God, that giveth to all men liberally, and upbraideth not; and it shall be given him." Through the difficult situations that the deacons and I faced in our ministry, we constantly cried out for God's wisdom in dealing with the matters. He answered our prayer, and we can look back with great joy in the way God directed our path through those stormy days. There are many promises in the Bible that we may claim during difficult days. I have learned to rely on the promises of God when situations seem impossible. One of the promises that has helped me through difficult days is I Corinthians 10:13: "There hath no temptation taken you but such as is common to man: but God is faithful, who will not suffer you to be tempted above that ye are able; but will with the temptation also make a way to escape, that ye may be able to bear it." God will not bring more into our lives than we can bear with His strength. He will give us victory if we patiently wait on Him (Psalm 27:13-14).

God's Word brings comfort during times of trials. I have counseled many people to meditate in the Psalms during difficult days. In God's providence, I was reading through the Psalms every month during this most trying year in our ministry. There are many Psalms that promise strength and comfort. I have listed just a few here.

I will both lay me down in peace, and sleep: for thou, Lord, only makest me dwell in safety.
Psalm 4:1

Lord my God, in thee do I put my trust: save me from all them that persecute me, and deliver me.
Psalm 7:1

But I have trusted in thy mercy; my heart shall rejoice in thy salvation.
Psalm 13:5

Preserve me, O God: for in thee do I put my trust.
Psalm 16:1

I will love thee, O Lord, my strength. The Lord is my rock, and my fortress, and my deliverer; my God, my strength, in whom I will trust; my buckler, and the horn of my salvation, and my high tower. I will call upon the Lord, who is worthy to be praised: so shall I be saved from mine enemies.
Psalm 18:1-3

As for God, his way is perfect: the word of the Lord is tried: he is a buckler to all those that trust in him. For who is God save the Lord? or who is a rock save our God? It is God that girdeth me with strength, and maketh my way perfect.
Psalm 18:30-32

The Lord is my shepherd; I shall not want. He maketh me to lie down in green pastures: he leadeth me beside the still waters. He restoreth my soul: he leadeth me in the paths of righteousness for his

name's sake. Yea, though I walk through the valley of the shadow of death, I will fear no evil: for thou art with me; thy rod and thy staff they comfort me.
Psalm 23:1-4

The Lord is my light and my salvation; whom shall I fear? the Lord is the strength of my life; of whom shall I be afraid?
Psalm 27:1

Trust in the Lord, and do good; so shalt thou dwell in the land, and verily thou shalt be fed. Delight thyself also in the Lord; and he shall give thee the desires of thine heart. Commit thy way unto the Lord; trust also in him; and he shall bring it to pass.
Psalm 37:3-5

I waited patiently for the Lord; and he inclined unto me, and heard my cry. He brought me up also out of an horrible pit, out of the miry clay, and set my feet upon a rock, and established my goings.
Psalm 40:1-2

God is our refuge and strength, a very present help in trouble. ... Be still, and know that I am God: I will be exalted among the heathen, I will be exalted in the earth.
Psalm 46:1, 10

What time I am afraid, I will trust in thee. In God I will praise his word, in God I have put my trust; I will not fear what flesh can do unto me.
Psalm 56: 3-4

From the end of the earth will I cry unto thee, when my heart is overwhelmed: lead me to the rock that is higher than I.
Psalm 61:2

My soul, wait thou only upon God; for my expectation is from him. He only is my rock and my salvation: he is my defence; I shall not be moved.
Psalm 62:5-6

My flesh and my heart faileth: but God is the strength of my heart, and my portion for ever.
Psalm 73:26

But thou, O Lord, art a God full of compassion, and gracious, long-suffering, and plenteous in mercy and truth. O turn unto me, and have mercy upon me; give thy strength unto thy servant, and save the son of thine handmaid. Shew me a token for good; that they which hate me may see it, and be ashamed: because thou, Lord, hast holpen me, and comforted me.
Psalm 86:15–17

Help me, O Lord my God: O save me according to thy mercy: That they may know that this is thy hand; that thou, Lord, hast done it.
Psalm 109:26–27

He shall not be afraid of evil tidings: his heart is fixed, trusting in the Lord. His heart is established, he shall not be afraid, until he see his desire upon his enemies.
Psalm 112:7–8

Therefore is my spirit overwhelmed within me; my heart within me is desolate. I remember the days of old; I meditate on all thy works; I muse on the work of thy hands.
Psalm 143:4–5

Happy is he that hath the God of Jacob for his help, whose hope is in the Lord his God.
Psalm 146:5

Great is our Lord, and of great power: his understanding is infinite. The Lord taketh pleasure in them that fear him, in those that hope in his mercy.
Psalm 147:5, 11

During this challenging year I was reading five Psalms a day and thereby meditating on all 150 Psalms each month. I encourage people to do this, whether they are going through trials or not. The Psalms bring comfort, encouragement, and counsel to God's children and servants. I know they met a need in my life during difficult days.

One final promise that I claimed was given to us from the apostle Paul in II Corinthians 12:9: "And he said unto me, my grace is sufficient for thee: for my strength is made perfect in weakness. Most gladly therefore will I glory in my infirmities, that the power of Christ may rest upon me." Without God's grace where would any of us be? We are saved by grace; we are sanctified by grace; and we are sustained by grace. John Newton put it well when he wrote, "Amazing Grace how sweet the sound that saved a wretch like me."

Jim Berg, in his book *Changed into His Image*, gives four stabilizing truths for trouble. I have expanded upon those four and used the acrostic G.R.A.C.E. to remind myself of how to deal with difficulties.

G – Reminds me that God's *grace* is sufficient (II Corinthians 12:9).
R – Reminds me that God's *reason* is Christlikeness (Romans 8:29).
A – Tells me that God's *answers* are in the Bible (Romans 15:4).
C – Reminds me that God's *compassion* is constant (Jeremiah 31:3).
E – Encourages me with the fact that God's *escape* is promised
    (I Corinthians 10:13).

In difficult times, these promises can give comfort and strength.

A song that I have sung often during difficult days is "Rejoice in the Lord." It was written shortly after Ron Hamilton lost one of his eyes to cancer. However, through this trial a new ministry was established as Ron created the character "Patch the Pirate." Not only did God bring Ron through the difficulties, but He brought him through with a song and an expanded ministry. This is a wonderful testimony for all of us who deal with the trials of life. The words of "Rejoice in the Lord" give great instruction and hope.

> *God never moves without purpose or plan*
> *When trying His servant and molding a man.*
> *Give thanks to the Lord though your testing seems long;*
> *In darkness He giveth a song.*
>
> *I could not see through the shadows ahead;*
> *So I looked at the cross of my Savior instead.*
> *I bowed to the will of the Master that day;*
> *Then peace came and tears fled away.*

Now I can see testing comes from above;
God strengthens His children and purges in love.
My Father knows best, and I trust in His care;
Through purging more fruit I will bear.

(Chorus)

Oh, Rejoice in the Lord. He makes no mistake.
He knoweth the end of each path that I take.
For when I am tried and purified,
I shall come forth as gold.

THE PROPER PROCEDURES FOR DEALING WITH DIFFICULTIES

Seeking private reconciliation

Problems come from people; therefore, in dealing with problems, we must deal with people. God has told us in Matthew 18:15, "Moreover if thy brother shall trespass against thee, go and tell him his fault between thee and him alone: if he shall hear thee, thou hast gained thy brother." When we have been offended by a brother or sister in Christ, we have a responsibility to go to that person and talk with him or her alone about the situation. It is not right for us to discuss the situation with other people until we have discussed it with the person directly involved. The goal is to get it worked out between the two of us. A problem I see too often is that people get others involved before they go to the offender alone. Instead of dealing with the problem, they create an even greater problem—gossip or, possibly, even slander. Some have even used "prayer" as a means to sin, when they share a "prayer request" about someone against whom they have an offense.

We also have the responsibility to go to a brother or sister in Christ who may have a sin problem that needs to be corrected. Galatians 6:1 says, "Brethren, if a man be overtaken in a fault, ye which are spiritual, restore such a one in the spirit of meekness; considering thyself, lest thou also be tempted." We read in Proverbs, "Faithful are the wounds of a friend; but the kisses of an enemy are deceitful" (27:6). A faithful friend will always confront sin, but someone who calls himself a friend and overlooks sin is really an enemy. In our local churches, it is important for pastors, deacons, and members of the congregation to go to individuals with problems and talk with them personally and privately.

The Bible also tells us that if we know of a person who is offended with us, we have the responsibility to go and seek reconciliation. "Therefore if thou bring thy gift to the altar, and there rememberest that thy brother hath ought against thee; leave there thy gift before the altar, and go thy way; first be reconciled to thy brother, then come and offer thy gift" (Matthew 5:23-24). Not only do we have the responsibility to talk to a person who has offended us, but we must also talk to a person whom we have offended. I believe this should include people who believe that they have something against us, even if it is only a misunderstanding on their part.

As a pastor I have had this happen several times. A church member will inform me that another person is upset about something that I said or did. The person has not come to me with the problem but is talking to others in a way that he or she should not. Not only do we have the responsibility to talk to people when they have offended us, but we must also talk to them if we know they are holding an offense against us. The goal is not to criticize that person, but rather to correct the problem by going to the person directly. I have traveled great distances to meet with individuals that have "ought against" me for the purpose of seeking reconciliation. My biblical responsibility is "if it be possible, as much as lieth in you, live peaceably with all men" (Romans 12:18). It is not just the responsibility of the pastor to seek peace, but it is also the responsibility of the deacons and every member of the body of Christ. Jesus said, "Blessed are the peacemakers: for they shall be called the children of God" (Matthew 5:9).

Practicing church discipline

As a pastor I have tried to deal with private sins privately (Proverbs 17:9). Problems within the local body of believers should be handled privately in most situations. However, in Matthew 18:17 we are told that it is sometimes necessary to "tell it unto the church." I have learned that it is better to deal with things publicly when necessary, rather than to have gossip running uncontrolled throughout the church, community, and sometimes even throughout the nation.

When sin becomes public knowledge, sometimes public restoration is necessary. This is part of Proverbs 28:13: "He that covereth his sins shall not prosper: but whoso confesseth and forsaketh them shall have mercy." It is also "providing for honest things, not only in the sight of the Lord, but also in the sight of men" (II Corinthians 8:21). Many people have come to me as their pastor and have confessed private sins such as covetousness, pride, pornography, infidelity, bitterness, etc. I have dealt with these people privately, or in as narrow a circle of others as possible, and I have kept confidentially between myself and them. Sometimes, when sins have become publicly known, I have encouraged the individual to let his or her repentance and restoration be public also. Sins such as divorce, pregnancy out of wedlock, embezzlement, and even gossip have had to be dealt with publicly because the information was known by a large number of people. We usually do this at the end of our Wednesday night service. This is when the faithful folks attend and when we have the fewest outsiders. Rumors are eliminated, or at least reduced, when we speak the truth in love from the pulpits of our local churches.

One other situation requires public knowledge, the situation of a person who does not repent when confronted about a sin problem. Such a situation must be dealt with publicly so that the entire congregation can lovingly confront the offender, continuing to seek reconciliation and restoration of this person with the local body of believers. The primary passage dealing with church discipline is found in the book of Matthew:

> *Moreover if thy brother shall trespass against thee, go and tell him his fault between thee and him alone: if he shall hear thee, thou hast gained thy brother. But if he will not hear thee, then take with thee one or two more, that in the mouth of two or three witnesses every word may be established. And if he shall neglect to hear them, tell it unto the church: but if he neglect to hear the church, let him be unto thee as an heathen man and a publican.*
> Matthew 18:15-17

When a Christian brother or sister attempts to deal with a situation personally and privately but does not get reconciliation, then it is time to bring in another Christian to help. Sometimes people will want a deacon or pastoral staff member to be this second person. However, in most local churches there are many mature believers who are very capable of helping to solve problems and to reconcile brethren. If the second person is not able to bring the problem to resolution, then I believe it is time for a pastor to get involved, especially since some situations may need to be dealt with before the church. A pastor needs to have full understanding of the problem and must make every effort to solve the problem before it becomes a church discipline matter. The goal is always confession, reconciliation, and restoration. When this is accomplished, the matter can and should be dropped. Forgiveness is the pattern of our Lord Jesus Christ and should be our pattern, as well (Matthews 18:21-35).

When brethren, following Matthew 18:15-16, cannot get a problem solved among themselves, then the church must get involved in the situation. It is the responsibility of the pastor and deacons to determine which cases could require presentation before the church. I Corinthians 5:11-13, Philippians 2:14-15, and Proverbs 6:16-19 show us that the following offenses require church discipline if not corrected personally and privately:

- Fornication – Any sexual sin
- Coveting – An obsession in desiring that which does not rightfully belong to one, even to the point of doing wrong to get it
- Idolatry – Worship that only God should receive
- Railing – Criticism that divides the church
- Drunkenness – Including use of mind-altering drugs
- Extortion – Improper gain by use of threat
- False Witness – Spreading lies
- Sowing Discord – Spreading disunity among the brethren
- Murmuring – Spreading anger or discontentment

The following steps should be taken in dealing with an offending brother in the church:

1. A member who finds an offense with his brother shall confront that brother personally and privately. The goal should be to work toward a resolution between the two individuals (Matthew 18:15).
2. If the issue cannot be resolved, then the one initiating the restoration attempt shall go again, taking one or more witnesses (Matthew 18:16).

3. Upon continued lack of resolution, the matter shall be brought before the pastor and the deacons as the elected representatives of the church (Matthew 18:17, Acts 6:1-7). The deacons shall examine the charge, allowing the involved members to appear and make their cases. If the deacons determine that the offense is valid as a matter requiring church discipline and that there is still no resolution, they shall direct the pastor to continue.

4. The pastor shall inform the offending member of the decision of the deacons and give him a list of offenses before he is brought before the church.

5. Then the case shall be presented to the church for exclusion of the offending brother from membership, so that God may deal with the offender (I Corinthians 5:13).

It must be remembered that church discipline is not intended to punish the members, but rather to accomplish the following three things:

1. To ensure that God is glorified in the church
2. To restore members who are in sin
3. To warn others of the consequences of sin

At our church we have had the joy of seeing many members who were church disciplined come to repentance of their sin, asking for forgiveness publicly before the church, and being restored to fellowship with the membership. I have had the joy of marrying several couples who were divorced, disciplined, reconciled, and remarried to each other. Remember, "With men this is impossible; but with God all things are possible" (Matthew 19:26).

In I Corinthians 5, the Apostle Paul had to rebuke the Corinthian church for not practicing church discipline in the body. If he visited many churches today, he would have to give the same rebuke. It is never easy to discipline, whether it be with your children, or within your church (Hebrews 12:11). However, the Bible is clear on this subject, and church discipline must be practiced in order for a local church to be pure, growing, and blessed of God.

Dealing with accusations against the pastor

Pastors, like any church members, are susceptible to sin and may need loving confrontation. Additionally, pastors, even more than most church members, are subject to being misunderstood, misrepresented, or maligned. Scripture therefore provides both special protection and special accountability for the pastor: "Against an elder receive not an accusation, but before two or three witnesses. Them that sin rebuke before all, that others also may fear" (I Timothy 5:19-20). There is a special protection—there must be at least two witnesses to bring a charge against a pastor. There is also a sobering accountability—his sins on the level of those in I Corinthians 5 cannot be privately confessed and forgiven; they must be a matter of public rebuke.

I have had to practice this admonition in our local church and have had to help other local churches do it, as well. Pastoral infidelity cannot be tolerated if we want the church to be pure and holy, thereby receiving the blessing of God. Pastoral sin is public sin and needs to be dealt with publicly.

To bring an accusation against a pastor, an individual must practice Matthew 18, just as he would toward any other member of the church. Hopefully the situation can be corrected between the pastor and the church member at the one-on-one level. I have seen that accomplished numerous times in my ministry. However, if it cannot be settled at that level, then two or three witnesses should talk to the pastor about the situation. At this time I think it is wise for the chairman of the deacons to be in the meetings so that he can hear the specifics of the charges. Listening to the complaint, he may be able to determine whether it is a matter that needs to go to the deacons or whether it should be dismissed without the other deacons being involved.

Twice in my many years of pastoring I have had an accusation brought against me before the deacons of our church. In one instance two people brought the accusation; the other time it was three. Both times the accusation was first expressed to me and then to our deacons. The deacons listened to the accusations brought by two or three witnesses to determine the legitimacy of the charges. After hearing the accusations and my explanation, both times the accusation was dropped by the deacons. I have never been afraid, as a pastor, to let an accusation be brought to the deacons. However, I have discouraged people from doing so, since I know how a person may be viewed if they bring a false accusation against the pastor in front of the deacons who are serving faithfully with him. My goal in the ministry is always unity among the brethren (Psalm 133:1). Once an accusation is brought before the deacons and rejected, many times the accuser will feel rejected as well and will leave the church. Sad to say, that happened both times that accusations were brought against me.

Sometimes the accuser may want to go before the church even after the deacons have rejected his accusation against the pastor. This should not be allowed since it is the deacons' responsibility in their service to the church to determine the legitimacy of the charge. Sometimes the accuser will start going to the church, person by person, when he is not allowed the opportunity to address them as a body. If this takes place, the deacons should confront the individual for his railing and divisive spirit, because he is sowing discord among the brethren. If he continues to persist in his accusations, he should be church disciplined publicly and put out of the church. God hates the sowing of discord among the brethren, and we who protect God's church must hate it as well (Proverbs 6:19) while still loving the offending brother and seeking his restoration.

If the accusations against a pastor prove to be true, however, the pastor should be confronted by the deacons and required to apologize personally to any individuals affected and publicly to the church. One of the responsibilities of deacons in serving the local church is to hold a pastor accountable. If an offense disqualifies the pastor from effective leadership in the local church, he should be asked to resign from his position. From the I Timothy 3:2-7 passage on the qualifications for the pastor, consider especially the phrase, "Moreover, he *must* have a good report of them that are without." A wise pastor will graciously resign when he has disqualified himself from an effective ministry with a local congregation of people. If the pastor has committed adultery, he has disqualified himself permanently from a pastoral ministry. While the *sin* can be forgiven, the *reproach* will not go away (Proverbs 6:32-33). That pastor no longer has "a good report of them that are without." The Scripture teaches this, and experience reaffirms the truth. However, many other offenses that create a testimony problem in one location do not create the same issue in a new location. Thank the Lord, even pastors can receive the forgiveness of the Lord and of a church so that they can continue to be used in full-time Christian work elsewhere in the future. These situations must be handled biblically and prayerfully so that God's church is helped, not hurt. If a pastor clearly sins, he should be rebuked before the church so others may fear and avoid the same sinful action (I Timothy 5:20). Problems in personal lives or in a local church must be dealt with properly if we want to see God blessing individuals and local church ministries (Proverbs 28:13).

I have told our church many times that I do not want to be the cause of division. In a local work people come and people go—that is normal and necessary. However, the church is God's church; and I, as His undershepherd, never want to be the cause of God's church being hindered. I have used our deacons to help me discern God's will for my life, especially in these times of accusation. Proverbs 11:14 encourages this: "Where no counsel is, the people fall: but in the multitude of counsellors there is safety." Accusations or not, if the deacons thought it best for me to leave the church, I would leave. This assumes, of course, that the deacons were not wanting me to go so that the church could go liberal. I would stay and contend for doctrine and biblical principles in that case. However, I would not stay and contend because of individual personalities. God leads men to a church, and God leads men away from a church. Sometimes this leading comes through the counsel of others—and even through the behavior of others. My goal and the goal of the deacons should be to "trust in the Lord with all thine heart; and lean not unto thine own understanding. In all thy ways acknowledge him, and he shall direct thy paths" (Proverbs 3:5-6).

The book of I Peter tells us to not think it strange concerning the trials that come our way (I Peter 4:12). We are told "that the trial of your faith, being much more precious than of gold that perisheth, though it be tried with fire, might be found to praise and honor and glory at the appearing of Jesus Christ" (I Peter 1:7). Our goal in dealing with difficulties should always be to bring glory to our Lord Jesus Christ (I Corinthians 10:31) and to help ourselves and others become more like Jesus Christ (Romans 8:28-29). Remember, "Christ also suffered for us, leaving us an example, that ye should follow his steps" (I Peter 2:21). "If ye be reproached for the name of Christ, happy are ye; for the Spirit of glory and of God resteth upon you: on their part he is evil spoken of, but on your part he is glorified" (I Peter 4:14). We must remember to "be sober, be vigilant; because your adversary the devil, as a roaring lion, walketh about, seeking whom he may devour" (I Peter 5:8). The devil is always trying to destroy God's church, but fear not, Jesus Christ has promised to build His church (Matthew 16:18).

Remember that the attitude in which we handle difficulties is extremely important. We should always exhibit the fruit of the Spirit, "love, joy, peace, longsuffering, gentleness, goodness, faith, meekness, temperance" (Galatians 5:22-23). We should always be "speaking the truth in love" (Ephesians 4:15), and we should always be seeking to "overcome evil with good" (Romans 12:21). Remember the admonition in Scripture that came from the pen of the apostle Paul: "Let us therefore follow after the things which make for peace, and things wherewith one may edify another" (Romans 14:19).

There will be problems in life, and there will be problems in ministry. They cannot be avoided, and they must not be overlooked. God expects us to deal with the issues that come our way in a biblical, gracious, and compassionate manner (Ephesians 4:32). As we deal with difficulties God's way, His church is strengthened and His work is expanded.

CHAPTER REVIEW

1. Problems will come; do not be surprised.
2. See problems from God's perspective.
   - Rejoice in the providence of God.
   - Remember the purpose of God.
   - Rely on the promises of God.
3. Deal with problems God's way.
   - Seek private reconciliation first . . .
     - If someone has wronged you.
     - If someone continues in sin, disgracing the Lord, even if it is not an offense against you individually.
     - If someone believes (correctly or incorrectly) that you have wronged him or her.
   - Practice church discipline if necessary.
4. Deal wisely with accusations against a pastor:

- Require two or three witnesses for an accusation against a pastor.
- Pastors who sin are held to a higher level of accountability.

Difficulties will come: Dealing with them God's way brings joy!

GPS (GETTING THE PRINCIPLES SUMMARIZED)

Find answers to these questions in the chapter.

Introduction
1. How can you have a ministry without problems?

"The Spirit of the Lord Shall Lift up a Standard"
2. How can we have joy in difficulties?
3. What is God's purpose in allowing trials in our lives?
4. What area of the Scriptures is the first line of comfort, encouragement, and counsel during trials?

Seeking Private Reconciliation
5. Who has the responsibility to initiate reconciliation, the offender or the one offended?

Practicing Church Discipline
6. What rule governs when a person should make public confession of sin?
7. Is church discipline appropriate for all sin problems.

Dealing with Accusations against the Pastor
8. What special considerations does 1 Timothy 5:19-20 make in the case of accusations against a pastor.

Conclusion
9. What is our goal in dealing with difficulty?

APPles (Applying the Principles Practically)

Apply these ideas to your church. Discussion will often go beyond just the facts in the reading.

"When the Enemy Comes in like a Flood"
1. What is meant by "trust and verify"?
2. When should sin be made public outside the church?
3. What was the role of the deacons amid all of these problems?

APPENDICES

ELEVEN COMMANDMENTS FOR AN ENTHUSIASTIC TEAM

Taken from Ian Pearcy, Canadian Training Resources Group, Inc., 1984.

1. Help each other be right—not wrong.
2. Look for ways to make new ideas work—not for reasons they won't.
3. If in doubt—check it out; don't make negative assumptions about each other.
4. Help each other win.
5. Speak positively about each other and about your church at every opportunity, but give God the praise!
6. Maintain a good attitude no matter what the circumstance. Remember God is in control.
7. Act with initiative and courage as if all depends on you, but trust God with the results.
8. Do everything with enthusiasm.
9. Whatever you want—give it away.
10. Don't lose faith—never give up.
11. Have fun.

As leadership, it becomes your duty to make sure your attitudes and actions bring unity. If you think right relationships are difficult, just try working with wrong ones.

SAMPLE DEACONS MEETING AGENDA

Tri-City Ministries
Deacons Meeting Agenda
February 13, 1997
7:30 P.M.

Devotions and Prayer - Pastor Herbster
Reading of Minutes - Paul Swisher

Old Business:
1. Committee Selections
2. Widow Assignments
3. Development Report
4. Personnel Report
5. School Report

New Business:
1. Junior High Re-zoning
2. Communication Towers
3. Building Fund Giving
4. Evangelistic Effort
5. New Members Assigned
6. Next Meeting:
   March 13, 1997
   Devotions -

Appendix 3

SAMPLE DEACON CANDIDATE QUESTIONNAIRE

Name _____

Date _____

Home Address _____

Phone Number _____

1. Please list names and ages of the members of your family
   • Wife
   • Children
2. Read I Timothy 3:8-13. Do you scripturally qualify to be a deacon and are you willing to serve in that position for the next three years?
3. Please relate your salvation testimony.
4. Read Acts 6:1-4. What do you believe is the scriptural function of a deacon?
5. Please list your priorities in life.
6. How would you counsel a member of the congregation who had a complaint with someone in authority in the church?
7. Please state your position regarding the academic ministries at Tri-City (Tri-City Christian School).
8. Have you read and are you in agreement with the church Constitution and By-Laws including the Statement of Faith?
9. Are you currently living in accord with the church Standards of Conduct for leaders (enclosed)?

10. Have you, or has your wife, ever been divorced?
11. Do you have regular Bible study and prayer?
12. Do you lead your family in regular devotions?
13. Would you oppose the participation of the church in a ecumenical or charismatic program?
14. Do you belong to the Masonic Lodge or any other lodge having religious overtones?
15. Do you believe your wife and children are submissive to your leadership?

(The actual form has several spaces under "children" and leaves plenty of space for the candidate to write his answers to questions 2-15.)

Appendix 4

SAMPLE STANDARDS OF CONDUCT

The following Standards of Conduct are designed to encourage each person involved at this level of responsibility and leadership to watch carefully concerning matters of Christian testimony.

It is understood and agreed to that those at this level of leadership should by God's grace adhere to the following:

1. Faithful attendance to the services of Tri-City Baptist Church. This includes Sunday school, Sunday morning church services, Sunday evening services, Wednesday evening services and any other special meetings such as revivals, missions conference, etc.

2. Faithful attendance to the regular worker meetings in your ministry. If there is a conflict with another meeting, the pastor responsible for your specific area of ministry will determine which of the two meetings you should attend.

3. Faithful in visitation. All workers in our ministry are expected to be a continual witness for Christ. Each worker is expected to spend time visiting. Phone calling, although it is important, will not substitute for spending time in personal visitation.

4. Faithful in tithing to this local church. Where a person's treasure is determines where his heart is. You can give without loving, but you can't love without giving.

5. Faithfulness in being holy as He is holy. There are certain habits and activities more readily bringing criticism or

reproach to the cause of Christ, and therefore, abstinence from the following activities or habits is required:

- Any form of alcoholic beverage
- The use of tobacco in any form
- Dancing
- Attending movies
- Suggestive or immodest apparel
- Swearing
- Men must have a neat hair cut that is in accord with the Christian school code.

6. Faithful in demonstrating loyalty to the entire program of this local church.

This would include the careful watch of one's tongue. If a question or problem arises, go to the person directly in charge of the situation. If the problem is not resolved to your satisfaction, you should talk to the Pastor. Remember, a critical spirit is a divisive spirit.

SAMPLE CHURCH CONSTITUTION AND BY-LAWS

Since 1969 the Christian Law Association has been providing free legal assistance to Bible-believing churches and Christians who are experiencing difficulty in practicing their faith. Some legal problems can be avoided by clearly stating the position of the church in the church constitution and bylaws, a document which is available to people as they consider membership in the church.

We thank Dr. David Gibbs III for permission to print the CLA sample constitution. Some elements of the constitution, such as the statement of faith, are likely to be adjusted by any church, including that of the authors, to reflect God's leading in the individual local church. However, many legal pitfalls can be avoided by accessing the wisdom that the CLA has gained from more than forty years of defending churches and individual Christians.

For further information, contact the Christian Law Association at *ChristianLaw.org*.

CHURCH CONSTITUTION
& Ministry Bylaws

(Annotated by attorneys for the Christian Law Association)

INTRODUCTION

Every church, whether incorporated or unincorporated, must have an operational document. This is the internal ministry document that sets forth how the organization will operate, *i.e.*, the purposes of the organization, the election of officers, when organizational meetings will be held, if and how members will be admitted, etc. This document is commonly known as the bylaws, but may be known as the constitution or the constitution and bylaws. The bylaws need not be submitted to any governmental agency and should be written to reflect the specific needs and practices of the ministry. Whatever the name, this document governs the operation of the church.

In most instances, when a dispute as to the authority and duties of church officers or other governing body is taken to court, the court will look to the organization's bylaws to determine whether or not that officer or the voting members acted within the scope of his or their duties. For legal purposes, the set of bylaws is the organization's most important document because it sets out in detail the internal workings of the organization. It is vital that this document be prepared properly and that it include all the protections available for the organization to safeguard against many of the lawsuits that are being filed against religious organizations today. Courts generally hold that a member who joins a church with knowledge of the bylaws has agreed to be bound by the bylaws—even to those with which they may disagree

The church bylaws (and all of their amendments) must be kept in a church office file that is readily accessible. *Readily accessible* means that the church bylaws is not stored in an attic, a basement, or away from the premises of the church. If the bylaws cannot be placed on the pastor's desk within five minutes of the request, the document is not readily accessible. The members that are to be subject to the bylaws should either be given their own copy or should be given notice as to where on the ministry property they may review the bylaws. A court will not hold a member to bylaws of which he had no notice.

Each state has enacted laws establishing rules by which ministries incorporated as nonprofit corporations will be governed if it has no bylaws or if the bylaws do not speak to a specific issue. It is important that your organization at least consider all the issues presented in the Sample Church Bylaws that follow. The organization may then decide that its specific method of operation does not necessitate the inclusion of a section included in the Sample. For instance, many religious corporations, such as independently operated Christian schools, do not have members. If such is the case, that ministry's document should **not** include the membership bylaws found in the Christian Law Association's Sample Church Bylaws.

While a church or other ministry may omit provisions that do not apply to it, the organization will need at least some form of the majority of provisions included in CLA's Sample Church Bylaws to avoid having a court subject the ministry to the state's nonprofit corporation rules. For instance, if the church bylaws fail to provide for the amount and method of notice to call an organization meeting, and the amount and method of notice becomes an issue for the organization, a court will use the state's provisions to establish the amount and method of a meeting notice. The organization may set whatever operational rules it wishes, but its failure to do so would force a court to impose the state's rules as a default position in the event of a dispute that ends in court proceedings.

At the Christian Law Association, our hope and prayer is that this booklet will better enable ministry leaders to understand the church constitution and bylaws. Specific questions not covered by this booklet should be referred to the attorneys for your ministry or to attorneys for the Christian Law Association at (727) 399-8300.

FREQUENTLY ASKED QUESTIONS ABOUT THE MINISTRY CONSTITUTION AND BYLAWS

Q: **Must the church file its constitution and bylaws or any amendments with the state secretary of state or any other government office?**

A: No. This document is for internal use only, and you should not send the constitution or any amendments to the secretary of state's office. If you do so and the state does file the bylaws, they become a public record open to public review. You may need to provide a copy of the document if the ministry is applying to a government office for an exemption or a permit. For instance, you will need to supply a copy to the IRS if you file an IRS Form 1023 Application for Recognition of Exemption Under Section 501(c)(3) of the Internal Revenue Code or when you apply in some states for property tax exemption.

Q: **How do we amend the current church constitution?**

A: To amend the current church constitution, follow the amendment procedures set out in the current church bylaws. In CLA's Sample Bylaws, the procedure for amendment provides that the provisions may be amended by a majority vote of the members present and voting at any regular church administration meeting, provided that the amendment has been submitted in writing and announced from the pulpit (14) days before the vote is taken.

Q: **How do we adopt an entirely new church constitution?**

A: If your current bylaws contain a procedure for adopting an entirely new set of bylaws, follow that procedure. If it contains no such procedures, you may follow the procedures for amending or revising bylaws set out in your current bylaws. In CLA's Sample Bylaws, the procedure for amendment provides that the provisions may be amended by a majority vote of the members present and voting at any regular church administration meeting, provided that the revision or amendment has been submitted in writing and announced from the pulpit (14) days before the vote is taken.

Q: **Do we need to take any action to repeal old bylaws when we amend them?**

A: A vote to amend a bylaw or bylaws automatically operates to repeal or to supersede all previous versions of the amended bylaw or bylaws. The same is true if you adopt a whole new set of bylaws. You need not take an additional vote to repeal the old bylaws.

Q: **May we prevent the bylaws from ever being changed by providing in our bylaws that part or all may never be amended?**

A: No. Although the church may include a provision that a particular bylaw can never be amended, the provision has no legal effect. You need to remember that whatever the organization adopts, it may always amend or repeal using the bylaws' amendment procedure. Stating that a bylaw can never be amended does emphasize its importance to the church and may cause members to pause before changing it. Nevertheless, the limitation will not legally prohibit a later amendment to the bylaw.

Q: **May we vote to dismiss or otherwise discipline members who are not in the meeting in which the vote is to be taken?**

A: Only if those members have been given proper notice of the meeting and have chosen not to attend. In CLA's Sample Church Bylaws, a member may be disciplined by following the procedures established in Section 3.04 (A) – (H). When steps (A) through (D) have been completed and it has been determined that a member is unrepentant and must be disciplined, the discipline committee recommends to the members of the church that disciplinary action be taken against the offending member. Section 3.04(E) requires the disciplinary action to be taken by "a majority vote of the membership present at a meeting called for the purpose of considering disciplinary action." A church discipline meeting is a special meeting. Therefore, the procedures for calling a special meeting established in Section 6.03 must be complied with, requiring the pastor to call the meeting by giving notice of the meeting and its purpose "from the pulpit at least one Sunday and not less than one week prior to said meeting." If, under CLA's Sample Church Bylaws, the meeting is properly called (by the pastor) and noticed (on at least one Sunday from the pulpit at least a week in advance), a vote to dismiss the offending members will be effective in the event the vote is ever challenged, even if the member chose not to attend the special meeting.

Q: **If one of the rules in our bylaws is not working for the church, may we just ignore it and amend it later?**

A: No, you may not just ignore bylaws. You may create any rules for the operation of the organization that you wish, but if you have a bylaw, you must follow it. The First Amendment to the United States Constitution prohibits courts from reviewing the ecclesiastical actions of a church in such matters as the selection and discipline of members and the selection or termination of the pastor. Courts may, however, review whether the church followed its own procedures for the selection and discipline of members and the selection or termination of the pastor. Once the court finds out that the church followed its own procedures, the court must cease all further review of the church proceedings.

SAMPLE CHURCH BYLAWS

(Annotated by attorneys for the Christian Law Association)

ARTICLE 1 – NAME AND PURPOSE

Section 1.01—Name
This congregation of believers shall be known as the _____
_____.

Section 1.02—Purpose[4]

This congregation is organized as a church exclusively for charitable, religious, and educational purposes within the meaning of Section 501 (c) (3) of the Internal Revenue Code of 1986 (or the corresponding provision of any future United States Revenue Law), including, but not limited to, for such purposes, the establishing and maintaining of religious worship, the building of churches, parsonages, schools, chapels, radio stations, television stations, rescue missions, print shops, daycare centers, and camps; the evangelizing of the unsaved by the proclaiming of the Gospel of the Lord Jesus Christ; the educating of believers in a manner consistent with the requirements of Holy Scripture, both in Sunday and weekday schools of Christian education; and the maintaining of missionary activities in the United States and any foreign country.

ARTICLE 2 – STATEMENT OF FAITH AND COVENANT

Section 2.01—Statement Of Faith[5]

The following comprise the Scriptural beliefs of this church and its members.

(A)   **The Holy Scriptures.** We believe the Holy Scriptures of the Old and New Testament to be the verbally and plenarily inspired

---

4 *The purpose provision should be broad in scope. Be sure it covers the full range of your present ministries and all possible future ministries yet does not overreach the purpose so as to violate your church's federal tax-exempt status. It should state what the church believes it is called to be and do for the Lord.*

5 *The ministry bylaws should set forth a statement of what the ministry believes about the traditional doctrinal areas of the faith, the doctrinal distinctives of the church, and its position on social matters such as separation, divorce and remarriage, and lawsuits between believers. The church bylaws should state what the version of the Bible is to be for the church.*
In addition, since other social issues create more litigation than others, it has become necessary for churches to declare in writing their positions on such issues as same-sex marriage, homosexuality, family relationships, human sexuality, and abortion. The church needs to spell out what its religious beliefs are on these issues to inform the members what is expected of them regarding their behavior. A published explanation can eliminate a multitude of problems before they arise if members understand the church's expectations for their behavior.

Word of God. The Scriptures are inerrant, infallible and God-breathed and, therefore, are the final authority for faith and life. The sixty-six books of the Old and New Testament are the complete and divine revelation of God to Man. The Scriptures shall be interpreted according to their normal grammatical-historical meaning, and all issues of interpretation and meaning shall be determined by the pastor. The King James Version of the Bible shall be the official and only translation used by the church. (2 Tim. 3:16-17; 2 Pet. 1:20-21)

(B)   **Dispensationalism.** We believe that the Scriptures interpreted in their natural, literal sense reveal divinely determined dispensations or rules of life which define man's responsibilities in successive ages. These dispensations are not ways of salvation, but rather are divinely ordered stewardships by which God directs man according to His purpose. Three of these dispensations—the law, the church, and the kingdom—are the subjects of detailed revelation in Scripture. (Gen. 1:28; 1 Cor. 9:17; 2 Cor. 3:9-18; Gal. 3:13-25; Eph. 1:10; 3:2-10; Col. 1:24-25, 27; Rev. 20:2-6)

(C)   **The Godhead.**   We believe in one triune God, eternally existing in three persons—Father, Son, and Holy Spirit—each co-eternal in being, co-identical in nature, coequal in power and glory, and having the same attributes and perfections. (Deut. 6:4; Matt. 28:19; John 14:10, 26; 2 Cor. 13:14)

(D)   **The Person and Work of Christ.**

1.   We believe that the Lord Jesus Christ, the eternal Son of God, became man, without ceasing to be God, having been conceived by the Holy Spirit and born of the virgin Mary, in order that He might reveal God and redeem sinful men. (Isa. 7:14; 9:6; Luke 1:35; John 1:1-2, 14; 2 Cor. 5:19-21; Gal. 4:4-5; Phil. 2:5-8)

2.   We believe that the Lord Jesus Christ accomplished our redemption through His death on the cross as a representative, vicarious, substitutionary sacrifice; and, that our justification is made sure by His literal, physical resurrection from the dead. (Acts 2:18-36; Rom. 3:24-25; Eph. 1:7; 1 Pet. 2:24; 1 Peter 1:3-5)

3.   We believe that the Lord Jesus Christ ascended to Heaven and is now exalted at the right hand of God where, as our High Priest, He fulfills the ministry of Representative, Intercessor, and Advocate. (Acts 1:9-10; Rom. 8:34; Heb. 9:24; 7:25; 1 John 2:1-2)

(E)   The Person and Work of the Holy Spirit.

1.   We believe that the Holy Spirit is a person who convicts the world of sin, of righteousness, and of judgment; and, that He is the Supernatural Agent in regeneration, baptizing all believers into the body of Christ, indwelling and sealing them unto the day of redemption. (John 16:8-11; Rom. 8:9; 1 Cor. 12:12-14; 2 Cor. 3:6; Eph. 1:13-14)

2.   We believe that He is the divine Teacher who assists believers to understand and appropriate the Scriptures and that it is the privilege and duty of all the saved to be filled with the Spirit. (Eph. 1:17-18; 5:18; 1 John 2:20, 27)

3.   We believe that God is sovereign in the bestowal of spiritual gifts to every believer. God uniquely uses evangelists, pastors, and teachers to equip believers in the assembly in order that they can do the work of the ministry. (Rom. 12:3-8; 1 Cor. 12:4-11, 28; Eph. 4:7-12)

4.   We believe that the sign gifts of the Holy Spirit, such as speaking in tongues and the gift of healing, were temporary. Speaking in tongues was never the common or necessary sign of the baptism or filling of the Holy Spirit. Ultimate deliverance of the body from sickness or death awaits the consummation of our salvation in the resurrection, though God frequently chooses to answer the prayers of believers for physical healing. (1 Cor. 1:22; 13:8; 14:21-22)

(F)   **The Total Depravity of Man.**   We believe that man was created in the image and likeness of God; but that in Adam's sin the human race fell, inherited a sinful nature, and became alienated from God. Man is totally depraved and, of himself, utterly unable to remedy his lost condition. (Gen. 1:26-27; Rom. 3:22-23; 5:12; 6:23; Eph. 2:1-3; 4:17-19)

(G)   **Salvation.**   We believe that salvation is the gift of God brought to man by grace and received by personal faith in the Lord Jesus Christ, Whose precious blood was shed on Calvary for the forgiveness of our sins. We believe that all sins, except blasphemy of the Holy Spirit, are forgivable. (Matt. 12:31-32; John 1:12; Eph. 1:7; 2:8-10; 1 Pet. 1:18-19; 1 John 1:9)

(H)   **The Eternal Security and Assurance of Believers.**

1.   We believe that all the redeemed, once saved, are kept by God's power and are thus secure in Christ forever. (John 6:37-40; 10:27-30; Rom. 8:1; 38-39; 1 Cor. 1:4-8; 1 Pet. 1:4-5)

2.   We believe that it is the privilege of believers to rejoice in the assurance of their salvation through the testimony of God's Word, which, however, clearly forbids the use of Christian liberty as an occasion to the flesh. (Rom. 13:13-14; Gal. 5:13; Titus 2:11-15)

(I)   **The Church**

1.   We believe that the local church, which is the body and the espoused bride of Christ, is solely made up of born-again persons. (1 Cor. 12:12-14; 2 Cor. 11:2; Eph. 1:22-23; 5:25-27)

2. We believe that the establishment and continuance of local churches is clearly taught and defined in the New Testament Scriptures. (Acts 14:27; 20:17, 28-32; 1 Tim. 3:1-13; Titus 1:5-11)

3. We believe in the autonomy of the local church free of any external authority or control. (Acts 13:1-4; 15:19-31; 20:28; Rom. 16:1, 4; 1 Cor. 3:9, 16; 5:4-7, 13; 1 Pet. 5:1-4)

4. We recognize water baptism and the Lord's Supper as the Scriptural ordinances of obedience for the church in this age. (Matt. 28:19-20; Acts 2:41-42; 8:36-38; 1 Cor. 11:23-26)

(J) **Separation.** We believe that all the saved should live in such a manner as not to bring reproach upon their Savior and Lord. God commands His people to separate from all religious apostasy, all worldly and sinful pleasures, practices, and associations, and to refrain from all immodest and immoderate appearances, piercings, and bodily markings. (Lev. 19:28; Rom. 12:1-2; 14:13; 1 Cor. 6:19-20; 2 Cor. 6:14-7:1; 2 Tim. 3:1-5; 1 John 2:15-17; 2 John 9-11)

(K) **The Second Advent of Christ.** We believe in that *blessed hope*, the personal, imminent return of Christ, Who will rapture His church prior to the seven-year tribulation period. At the end of the Tribulation, Christ will personally and visibly return with His saints, to establish His earthly Messianic Kingdom which was promised to the nation of Israel. (Ps. 89:3-4; Dan. 2:31-45; Zech. 14:4-11; 1 Thess. 1:10, 4:13-18; Titus 2:13; Rev. 3:10; 19:11-16; 20:1-6)

(L) **The Eternal State.**

1. We believe in the bodily resurrection of all men, the saved to eternal life, and the unsaved to judgment and everlasting punishment. (Matt. 25:46; John 5:28, 29; 11:25-26; Rev. 20:5-6, 12-13)

2.   We believe that the souls of the redeemed are, at death, absent from the body and present with the Lord, where in conscious bliss they await the first resurrection, when spirit, soul, and body are reunited to be glorified forever with the Lord. (Luke 23:43; 2 Cor. 5:8; Phil. 1:23; 3:21; 1 Thess. 4:16-17; Rev. 20:4-6)

3.   We believe that the souls of unbelievers remain, after death, in conscious punishment and torment until the second resurrection, when with soul and body reunited, they shall appear at the Great White Throne Judgment, and shall be cast into the Lake of Fire, not to be annihilated, but to suffer everlasting conscious punishment and torment. (Matt. 25:41-46; Mark 9:43-48; Luke 16:19-26; 2 Thess. 1:7-9; Jude 6-7; Rev. 20:11-15)

(M)   **The Personality of Satan.** We believe that Satan is a person, the author of sin and the cause of the Fall of Man; that he is the open and declared enemy of God and man; and that he shall be eternally punished in the Lake of Fire. (Job 1:6-7; Isa. 14:12-17; Matt. 4:2-11; 25:41; Rev. 20:10)

(N)   **Creation.** We believe that God created the universe in six literal, 24-hour periods. We reject evolution, the Gap Theory, the Day-Age Theory, and Theistic Evolution as unscriptural theories of origin. (Gen. 1-2; Ex. 20:11)

(O)   **Civil Government.** We believe that God has ordained and created all authority consisting of three basic institutions: 1) the home, 2) the church, and 3) the state. Every person is subject to these authorities, but all (including the authorities themselves) are answerable to God and governed by His Word. God has given each institution specific Biblical responsibilities and balanced those responsibilities with the understanding that no institution has the right to infringe upon the other. The home, the church, and the state are equal and sovereign in their respective Biblically assigned spheres of responsibility under God. (Rom. 13:1-7; Eph. 5:22-24; Heb. 13:17; 1 Pet. 2:13-14)

(P)   Human Sexuality.

1.   We believe that God has commanded that no intimate sexual activity be engaged in outside of a marriage between one man and one woman. We believe that any form of homosexuality, lesbianism, bisexuality, bestiality, incest, fornication, adultery, and pornography are sinful perversions of God's gift of sex. We believe that God disapproves of and forbids any attempt to alter one's gender by surgery or appearance. (Gen. 2:24; Gen. 19:5, 13; Gen. 26:8-9; Lev. 18:1-30; Rom. 1: 26-29; 1 Cor. 5:1; 6:9; 1 Thess. 4:1-8; Heb. 13:4)

2.   We believe that the only Scriptural marriage is the joining of one man and one woman. (Gen. 2:24; Rom. 7:2; 1 Cor. 7:10; Eph. 5:22-23)

(Q)   Family Relationships

1.   We believe that men and women are spiritually equal in position before God but that God has ordained distinct and separate spiritual functions for men and women in the home and the church. The husband is to be the leader of the home, and men are to be the leaders (pastors and deacons) of the church. Accordingly, only men are eligible for licensure and ordination by the church. (Gal. 3:28; Col. 3:18; 1 Tim. 2:8-15; 3:4-5, 12)

2.   We believe that God has ordained the family as the foundational institution of human society. The husband is to love his wife as Christ loves the church. The wife is to submit herself to the Scriptural leadership of her husband as the church submits to the headship of Christ. Children are an heritage from the Lord.

Parents are responsible for teaching their children spiritual and moral values and leading them, through consistent lifestyle example and appropriate discipline, including Scriptural corporal correction. (Gen. 1:26-28; Ex. 20:12; Deut. 6:4-9; Ps. 127:3-5; Prov. 19:18; 22:15; 23:13-14; Mk. 10:6-12; 1 Cor. 7:1-16; Eph. 5:21-33; 6:1-4, Col. 3:18-21; Heb. 13:4; 1 Pet. 3:1-7)

(R)   **Divorce and Remarriage.** We believe that God disapproves of and forbids divorce and intends marriage to last until one of the spouses dies. Divorce and remarriage is regarded as adultery except on the grounds of fornication. Although divorced and remarried persons or divorced persons may hold positions of service in the church and be greatly used of God for Christian service, they may not be considered for the offices of pastor or deacon. (Mal. 2:14-17; Matt. 19:3-12; Rom. 7:1-3; 1 Tim. 3:2, 12; Titus 1:6)

(S)   **Abortion.** We believe that human life begins at conception and that the unborn child is a living human being. Abortion constitutes the unjustified, unexcused taking of unborn human life. Abortion is murder. We reject any teaching that abortions of pregnancies due to rape, incest, birth defects, gender selection, birth or population control, or the physical or mental well being of the mother are acceptable. (Job 3:16; Ps. 51:5; 139:14-16; Isa. 44:24; 49:1, 5; Jer. 1:5; 20:15-18; Luke 1:44)

(T)   **Euthanasia.** We believe that the direct taking of an innocent human life is a moral evil, regardless of the intention. Life is a gift of God and must be respected from conception until natural death. Thus we believe that an act or omission which, of itself or by intention, causes death in order to eliminate suffering constitutes a murder contrary to the will of God. Discontinuing medical procedures that are extraordinary or disproportionate to the expected outcome can be a legitimate refusal of over-zealous treatment. (Ex. 20:13, 23:7; Matt. 5:21; Acts 17:28)

(U)   Love. We believe that we should demonstrate love for others, not only toward fellow believers, but also toward both those who are not believers, those who oppose us, and those who engage in sinful actions. We are to deal with those who oppose us graciously, gently, patiently, and humbly. God forbids the stirring up of strife, the taking of revenge, or the threat or the use of violence as a means of resolving personal conflict or obtaining personal justice. Although God commands us to abhor sinful actions, we are to love and pray for any person who engages in such sinful actions. (Lev. 19:18; Matt. 5:44-48; Luke 6:31; John 13:34-35; Rom. 12:9-10; 17-21; 13:8-10; Phil. 2:2-4; 2 Tim. 2:24-26; Titus 3:2; 1 John 3:17-18)

(V)   Lawsuits Between Believers. We believe that Christians are prohibited from bringing civil lawsuits against other Christians or the church to resolve personal disputes. We believe the church possesses all the resources necessary to resolve personal disputes between members. We do believe, however, that a Christian may seek compensation for injuries from another Christian's insurance company as long as the claim is pursued without malice or slander. (1 Cor. 6:1-8; Eph. 4:31-32)

(W)   Missions. We believe that God has given the church a great commission to proclaim the Gospel to all nations so that there might be a great multitude from every nation, tribe, ethnic group, and language group who believe on the Lord Jesus Christ. As ambassadors of Christ we must use all available means to go to the foreign nations and not wait for them to come to us. (Matt. 28:19-20; Mark 16:15; Luke 24:46-48; John 20:21; Acts 1:8; 2 Cor. 5:20)

(X)   Giving. We believe that every Christian, as a steward of that portion of God's wealth entrusted to him, is obligated to financially support his local church. We believe that God has established the tithe as a basis for giving, but that every Christian should also give other offerings sacrificially and cheerfully to the support of the church, the relief of those in need, and the spread of the Gospel. We believe that a Christian relinquishes all rights to direct the use of his tithe or offering once the gift has been made. (Gen. 14:20; Prov. 3:9-10; Acts 4:34-37; 1 Cor. 16:2; 2 Cor. 9:6-7; Gal. 6:6; Eph. 4:28; 1 Tim. 5:17-18; 1 John 3:17)

Section 2.02—Authority Of Statement of Faith

The Statement of Faith does not exhaust the extent of our faith. The Bible itself is the sole and final source of all that we believe. We do believe, however, that the foregoing Statement of Faith accurately represents the teaching of the Bible and, therefore, is binding upon all members. All literature used in the church shall be in complete agreement with the Statement of Faith.

Section 2.03—Covenant

Having been led, as we believe, by the Spirit of God, to receive the Lord Jesus Christ as our Savior, and on profession of our faith, having been baptized in the name of our Father, and of the Son, and of the Holy Ghost, we do now, in the presence of God, angels, and this assembly, most solemnly and joyfully enter into covenant with one another, as one body in Christ.

We engage, therefore, by the aid of the Holy Spirit, to walk together in Christian love; to strive for the advancement of this church in knowledge, holiness and comfort; to promote its prosperity and spirituality; to sustain its worship, ordinances, discipline and doctrines; to give it a sacred preeminence over all institutions of human origin; and to contribute cheerfully and regularly to the support of the ministry, the expenses of the church, the relief of the poor, and the spread of the Gospel through all nations.

We also engage to maintain family and private devotions; to religiously educate our children; to seek the salvation of our kindred, acquaintances, and all others; to walk circumspectly in the world; to be just in our dealings, faithful to our engagements, and exemplary in our deportment; to avoid all tattling, backbiting, and excessive anger; to abstain from such worldly amusements as watching ungodly movies, gambling, rock music, and dancing; to be free from all oath-bound secret societies and partnerships with unbelievers; to abstain from the sale or use of tobacco in any form, narcotic drugs, or intoxicating drink as a beverage; and to be zealous in our efforts to advance the Kingdom of our Savior.

We further engage to watch over one another in brotherly love; to remember each other in prayer; to aid each other in sickness and distress; to cultivate Christian sympathy in feeling and courtesy of speech; to be slow to take offense, but always ready for reconciliation, and mindful of the rules of our Savior, and to secure reconciliation without delay.

We moreover engage, that when we remove from this place, we will as soon as possible unite with some other church where we can carry out the spirit of this covenant and the principles of God's Word.

ARTICLE 3 – MEMBERSHIP[6]

Section 3.01—Qualifications For Membership

Upon a majority vote of the members present at any church service or meeting, membership shall be extended to all who have had and whose lives evidence a genuine experience of regeneration through faith in and acceptance of the Lord Jesus Christ as personal Savior; who renounce sin; who endeavor to live a consecrated life wholly unto the Lord; who fully subscribe to the Statement of Faith contained herein; who enter into the church covenant contained herein; who agree to submit to the authority of the church and its leaders as set forth herein; and upon compliance with any one of the following conditions:

---

6 *The church bylaws should carefully specify the qualifications for membership. Most churches will want the members to be believers who give full assent to the Statement of Faith and the Church Covenant and who have been baptized subsequent to conversion. The church bylaws should specifically set forth the procedures for admission to church membership. For example, may members be admitted at any service of the church? Does the church vote on the admission of members? Is it merely a voice vote? Is the membership subject to the prospective member completing a membership class or signing a statement of assent to the Statement of Faith and the Church Covenant? Also, do the church bylaws specifically set forth the basis for the termination of church membership?*

(A) By baptism (immersion) as a true believer in Christ Jesus as personal Savior;

(B) By letter of transfer from another Bible-believing church of like faith and practice, or other written statement of good standing from the prior church if the applicant has been baptized by immersion subsequent to a profession of faith;

(C) By testimony of faith, having been baptized by immersion; or

(D) By restoration, if having been removed from membership, upon majority vote of the congregation after confession is made publicly before the church membership of the sin or sins involved, and satisfactorily evidencing repentance to the pastor (or the board of deacons if the office of pastor is vacant).

SECTION 3.02—DUTIES OF A MEMBER

On becoming a member of this church, in addition to the covenant contained in Section 2.03, each member further covenants to love, honor, and esteem the pastor; to pray for him; to recognize his authority in spiritual affairs of the church; to cherish a brotherly love for all members of the church; to support the church in prayer, tithes, offerings and with other financial support as the Lord enables; and in accordance with Biblical commands, to support through a lifestyle walk affirming the beliefs and practices of the church.

Section 3.03—Privileges Of Membership[7]

(A) Only members at least eighteen years of age who are physically present at a duly called meeting of the church shall be entitled

---

7 *It is absolutely critical that the church limit the voting rights of a member to only those present. Our office has seen the damage that proxy and absentee voting can cause in a church. Many churches do not realize the danger until a decision is hijacked by a group of disgruntled members who choose to vote as a block even though they have not been to church in years. In one church dispute, both factions claimed to have the proxy for a mentally disabled member in a nursing home. Prohibiting absentee or proxy voting will eliminate such claims.*

to vote. There shall be no proxy or absentee voting. The eligible membership of the church has certain limited areas to exercise a vote. Members may not vote to initiate any church action, rather the vote of a member is to confirm and ratify the direction of the church as determined by the pastor and the board of deacons.

(B)   This congregation functions not as a pure democracy, but as a body under the headship of the Lord Jesus Christ and the direction of the pastor as the undershepherd with the counsel of the board of deacons. Determinations of the internal affairs of this church are ecclesiastical matters and shall be determined exclusively by the church's own rules and procedures. The pastor shall oversee and/or conduct all aspects of this church. The board of deacons shall give counsel and assistance to the pastor as requested by him.[8]

(C)   Membership in this church does not afford the members with any property, contractual, or civil rights based on principles of democratic government. Although the general public is invited to all of the church's worship services, the church property remains private property. The pastor (or in his absence, an individual designated by the board of deacons) has the authority to suspend or revoke the right of any person, including a member, to enter or remain on church property. If after being notified of such a suspension or revocation, the person enters or remains on church property, the person may, in the discretion of the pastor (or in his absence, an individual designated by the board of deacons), be treated as a trespasser.[9]

---

8 *Be sure your church bylaws state clearly that members have no contract, property, or civil legal rights in the property or other ministry affairs of the church. Some states invest members with these rights unless restricted by the bylaws.*

9 *The church bylaws should set forth any limitations on a member's right to inspect church records. We recommend that you minimize the access a member can have to church records. Imagine the impact and cost if an angry member demands that the church provide records from three to five years in the past. In some states, members have this right unless the bylaws restrict members' access to records. The following is the most restrictive access that is legally permissible.*

(D)   A member may inspect or copy the prepared financial statements of the church and the minutes of the proceedings of church meetings and of board meetings, provided he shall have made a written request upon the church and the church has received the written request at least five business days before the requested inspection date

    1.   A member may not, under any circumstances, inspect or copy any record relating to individual contributions to the church, the list of names and addresses of the church members, or the accounting books and financial records of the church.

    2.   The church may impose a reasonable charge, covering the costs of labor and material, for copies of any documents provided to the member before releasing the copies to the member.

Section 3.04—Discipline Of A Member[10]

(A)   There shall be a discipline committee consisting of the pastor and the board of deacons. These men shall have sole authority in determining heretical deviations from the Statement of Faith and violations of the church covenant. If the pastor or a deacon is the subject of a disciplinary matter, he shall not sit as a member of the discipline committee. The pastor and deacons shall be entitled to the same steps as other church members and be subject to the same discipline.

(B)   Members are expected to demonstrate special loyalty and concern for one another. When a member becomes aware of an offense of such magnitude that it hinders spiritual growth

---

10 *The church bylaws need to state the discipline process that a church will follow in dealing with an erring member. It is not sufficient merely to provide the Scripture references. The specific steps should be stated. Although in any discipline situation this outline should be followed to the letter, the discipline committee should be given the authority to determine whether and when the process has been properly followed.*

and testimony, he is to go alone to the offending party and seek to restore his brother. Before he goes, he should first examine himself. When he goes, he should go with a spirit of humility and have the goal of restoration.

(C)   If reconciliation is not reached, a second member, either a deacon or the pastor, is to accompany the one seeking to resolve the matter. This second step should also be preceded by self-examination and exercised in a spirit of humility with the goal of restoration.

(D)   If the matter is still unresolved after the steps outlined in subsections (B) and (C) have been taken, the discipline committee, as the church representatives Biblically responsible for putting down murmuring, shall hear the matter. If the matter is not resolved during the hearing before the discipline committee, the committee shall recommend to the members of the church that they, after self-examination, make an effort personally to go to the offending member and seek that member's restoration.

(E)   If the matter is still unresolved after the steps outlined in subsections (B), (C), and (D) have been taken, such members who refuse to repent and be restored are to be removed from the membership of the church upon a majority vote of the membership present at a meeting called for the purpose of considering disciplinary action.[11]

(F)   No matter may be heard by the discipline committee or the church unless the steps outlined in subsections (B) and (C) have been taken, except in the case of a public offense.

---

11 *Notice in the following provision that there is an allusion to a public offense. The determination of what is a public offense should be left to the discretion of the discipline committee. A public offense does not Biblically require the procedure of church discipline as normally laid out. Instead, the matter may be expedited to prevent any additional shame or contention within the church. For an example of Biblical discipline of a public offense, see 1 Corinthians 5.*

(G)   If an unrepentant offending party is removed from the church membership, all contact with him from that point forward (except by family members) must be for the sake of restoration.

(H)   The procedures provided in this section are based on Matt. 18:15-20; Rom. 16:17-18; 1 Cor. 5:1-13; 2 Cor. 2:1-11; Gal. 6:1; 1 Thess. 5:14; 2 Thess. 3:6, 10-15; 1 Tim. 5:19-20; and Titus 3:10-11.

Section 3.05—Transfer Of Membership

Members not under the disciplinary process of Section 3.04 may request that letters of transfer be sent to another church.

Section 3.06—Termination Of Membership

(A)   The membership of any individual member shall automatically terminate without notice if the member in question has not attended a regular worship service of the church in the preceding six months. Upon good cause being shown to the pastor, this provision for termination may be waived in the case of any individual member at the discretion of the pastor. [12]

---

12 *CLA strongly recommends that an automatic termination of membership for nonattendance be included in the bylaws. This provision will automatically, and without any further action from anyone, remove from the church membership rolls any person who has not attended a regular church service in the amount of time established by the church. Ideally, that period of time should be less than a year.*

We recommend against placing members in an "inactive" membership because of the problems this vague status causes. For instance, may those "inactive" members vote? If not, may they attend members only meetings? If so, may they have a say on the issue at hand? When they are present in a meeting in which a vote is taken, are they counted for purposes of determining whether a quorum is present?

It has been our experience that in most cases in which there is internal church dissension, members who have not attended for months appear and expect to have a say and/or vote in the matter. We should know that someone who has not attended any service in several months is upset at something. Providing for an automatic termination clears up any confusion as to who is eligible to

(B)   No member of this church may hold membership in another church. The membership of any individual member shall automatically terminate without notice if the member unites in membership with another church.

(C)   The membership of any individual member shall automatically terminate without notice if the member states that he or she is actively involved in any conduct described in Section 2.01(P) or files a lawsuit in violation of Section 2.01(V).[13]

(D)   No provision contained in this section shall be subject to or governed by the procedures regarding discipline of members set forth in Section 3.04.

(E)   A member may resign at any time, but no letter of transfer or written statement of good standing will be issued upon such resignation, except at the discretion of the pastor.

---

vote, attend members meetings, count for quorum purposes, or have a say in a members meeting. You may exclude from this termination provision such persons as college students, military personnel, shut-ins, missionaries, evangelists or others who are legitimately unable to regularly attend services.

13   The automatic termination of members who flaunt their sexual immorality spares the church the shame of having to "speak of those things which are done of them in secret" for discipline purposes. The automatic termination for "going to law against a brother" provides the church with protection against having to retain as a member an individual who is willing to harm the church by taking it to court. Because this provision is automatic, it avoids the charge of retaliation.

ARTICLE 4 – OFFICERS[14]

Section 4.01—church Officers

The church officers are pastor (see Section 5.01), deacon (see Section 5.02), minister of records (see Section 5.03), minister of finance (see Section 5.04). One person may hold two or more offices, except that of pastor. The pastor, from time to time as he deems appropriate, may appoint other church officers, subject to a confirmation vote of the church membership.

Section 4.02—Designation Of Corporate Officers

As an accommodation to legal relationships outside the church, the pastor shall serve as president of the corporation; the minister of records shall serve as secretary of the corporation; the minister of finances shall serve as treasurer of the corporation; and the chairman of the board of deacons shall serve as vice president of the corporation.

Section 4.03—Eligibility For Office

(A)   The church shall not install or retain an officer who fails to adhere to or expresses disagreement with the Statement of Faith. All church officers, upon request of the pastor, shall affirm their agreement with the Statement of Faith (as set forth in Article 2).

---

14 *Specify the procedures for selecting and removing the pastor and deacons. At a minimum, the church corporation needs to have a president, a secretary, and a treasurer. If the church prefers to use other titles, such as pastor or deacon, the bylaws need to identify the corporate function of the ministry name. For example, the pastor is generally stated to be the president of the corporation. The bylaws should also address the procedures for nominating and electing officers, the duties and terms of service for each officer, the procedure for removing an officer before the end of his elected term, and the procedure for filling a vacancy in an office.*

Do not create such an elaborate set of checks and balances that none of the church leadership has sufficient liberty to get anything done on behalf of the church and its ministries. The church leadership should have sufficient authority to effectively lead and conduct the ministries of the church.

(B)   All church officers must be approved initially and thereafter annually by the pastor in order for them to commence or continue in their offices.

(C)   Only church members are eligible for election or appointment to any church office or position.

Section 4.04—Terms Of Office

(A)   The relationship between the pastor and the church shall be permanent unless dissolved at the option of either party by the giving of a month's notice, or less by mutual consent. The calling of a pastor or severance of the relationship between the pastor and the church may be considered at any regular church administration meeting, provided notice to that effect shall have been given from the pulpit to the church two Sundays prior to said regular church administration meeting. A three-fourths majority of the eligible members present and voting shall be required to call a pastor or to sever the relationship between the pastor and the church. Disciplinary removal of the pastor from office automatically terminates his membership. A restoration to membership after disciplinary removal will be subject to the requirements of Section 3.01(D).

(B)   The term of service for all offices and positions in the church, except the pastor, shall be one year, at the expiration of which the officers may be re-elected or re-appointed.

(C)   A vacancy occurring in any office or board, except in the case of the pastor, may be filled at any regular church administration meeting.

(D)   All elected and appointed officers shall serve in their respective offices until their successors are duly elected or appointed.

(E)   Members of the board of deacons may be removed from office for unbiblical conduct, as determined by the other board members, upon a majority vote of the remaining members of the board of deacons.

Section 4.05—Election Of Officers

The annual election of officers by the church membership shall occur during the month of December at the annual church administration meeting.

Section 4.06—pastoral Oversight Of Officers And Staff

(A)   Subject to the approval of the church membership and on the condition that they shall become a member of the church upon assuming their duties, the pastor may hire associates and assistants to assist the him in carrying out his God-given responsibilities.

(B)   All church staff, whether paid or volunteer, shall be under the supervision of the pastor who has the sole authority to dismiss the same. No employee or volunteer shall be hired, appointed, or retained who fails to adhere to or expresses disagreement with the Statement of Faith.

ARTICLE 5 – DUTIES AND POWERS OF OFFICERS

Section 5.01—The pastor

(A)   The pastor shall preach the Gospel regularly and shall be at liberty to preach the whole counsel of the Word of God as the Lord leads him. He shall administer the ordinances of the church, act as moderator at all church meetings for the transaction of church matters, supervise the teaching ministries of the church, and tenderly watch over the spiritual interests of the membership.

(B)   The pastor shall appoint the members of the various committees at the annual church administration meeting. He shall serve as the president of the corporation. He shall publicly inform all newly elected officers of the particular function and the responsibilities of their respective offices. He shall extend the right hand of fellowship to all new members on behalf of the church and perform such other duties as generally appertain to such a position. The pastor shall be free to choose the means and methods by which he exercises the ministry that God has given him.

(C)   All appointments for public worship and Bible study and the arrangements thereof, including time and place and the use of the property belonging to the church for purposes other than the stated appointments, shall be under the control of the pastor.

Section 5.02—The Board Of Deacons

(A)   The board of deacons shall assist the pastor, in such manner as he shall request, in promoting the spiritual welfare of the church, in conducting the religious services, and in performing all other work of the church. They shall make provision for the observance of the ordinances of the church. They shall, if requested by the pastor, consider applications for church membership. They shall, in cooperation with the pastor, disburse the benevolence fund. They shall assist the pastor in visitation and all other evangelistic efforts of the church. The board of deacons shall assist the pastor in caring for the administrative needs of the church's various ministries as requested by the pastor. They shall provide the pulpit supply and choose a moderator for church meetings if the pastor is unavailable or the office of pastor is vacant. Upon the death, resignation, or dismissal of the pastor, the board of deacons may appoint a pulpit committee.

(B)   Immediately following the annual church administration meeting, the board of deacons shall assemble and elect, from their own number, a chairman who shall be vice president of the corporation, a vice chairman, and a secretary.[15]

(C)   The board of deacons shall constitute the board of trustees of the corporation.[16] The board of trustees shall exercise only the following specific powers, upon authorization by a majority vote of the members present at a duly called church administration meeting:

1.   To purchase, hold, lease, or otherwise acquire real and personal property on behalf of the church, and to take real and personal property by will, gift, or bequest on behalf of the church;

2.   To sell, convey, alienate, transfer, lease, assign, exchange, or otherwise dispose of, and to mortgage, pledge, or otherwise encumber the real and personal property of the church, to borrow money and incur indebtedness for the purpose and the use of the church; to cause to be executed, issued, and delivered for the indebtedness, in the name of the church, promissory notes, bonds, debentures, or other evidence of indebtedness; and to secure repayment by deeds of trust, mortgages, or pledges; and

3.   To exercise all powers necessary for the dissolution of the church corporation.

Section 5.03—The Minister Of Records

The minister of records shall:

---

15 *Someone must be able to legally act on behalf of the church. Normally those persons are known as trustees. They are so called because of their fiduciary duty to hold the church property in trust for the church. Whether these men are the deacons, elders, or another group of men, there must be a person or group that holds these powers.*

16 *Most states require a nonprofit corporation to have at least three directors (or trustees).*

(A)   Certify and keep at the office of the church, the original bylaws or a copy, including all amendments or alterations to the bylaws;

(B)   Keep at the place where the bylaws or a copy are kept a record of the proceedings of meetings of the board of deacons, with the time and place of holding, the notice of meeting given, the names of these present at the meetings;

(C)   Sign, certify, or attest documents as may be required by law;

(D)   See that all notices are duly given in accordance with the provisions of these bylaws. (In case of the absence or disability of the secretary, or his or her refusal or neglect to act, notice may be given and served by the pastor or by the chairman of the board of deacons.);

(E)   Be custodian of the records of the church, including the membership roll, baptisms, and certificates of ordination, licenses and commissions;

(F)   See that the reports, statements, certificates, and all other documents and records required by law are properly kept and filed;

(G)   Exhibit at all reasonable times to proper persons on terms provided by law the bylaws and minutes of proceedings of the board of deacons or the minutes of the meetings of the church members;

(H)   Keep an account of any special events in the life of the church which are of historical interest and give a report at the annual church administration meeting of the status of the church membership roll in the past year;

(I)   Keep all records at the office of the church and deliver them to any successor upon leaving office; and

(J)   Serve as the secretary of the corporation.

Section 5.04—The Minister Of Finance

The minister of finance shall:

(A)   Have charge and custody of, and be responsible for, all funds of the corporation, and deposit all funds in the name of the church in banks, trust companies, or other depositories as shall be selected by the pastor or the board of deacons;

(B)   Receive, and give receipt for all contributions, gifts, and donations to the church;

(C)   Disburse, or cause to be disbursed, the funds of the church as may be directed by the pastor, the board of deacons, or the budget adopted by the members of the church at the annual church administration meeting, taking proper vouchers for the disbursements;

(D)   Keep and maintain adequate and correct accounts of the church's properties and business transactions including account of its assets, liabilities, receipts, disbursements, and capital;

(E)   Make all expenditures of the church (except miscellaneous petty cash disbursements) by check;

(F)   When and as requested, render to the pastor and the board of deacons accounts of all his transactions as minister of finance and of the financial condition of the church;

(G)   Present a written report of itemized disbursements at the regular quarterly church administration meetings and make a general report for the year at the annual church administration meeting;

(H)   Keep all church financial records at the office of the church and deliver them to any successor upon leaving office; and

(I)   Serve as treasurer of the corporation.

Section 5.05—Associate pastors

Under the direction and guidance of the pastor, the associate pastor(s) of the church shall assist the pastor in carrying out the ministries of the church.

Section 5.06—Duties Of All Officers

(A)   All officers shall prepare a written report of their work for the annual church administration meeting and shall surrender all records in their possession to the minister of records at the close of their term of office to be filed as a permanent record of the work of the church. All records are the property of the church and must be kept in the church office.

(B)   Any officer who neglects his duties as outlined in the bylaws for a period of three months may be removed from his office, at the discretion of the pastor, and another may be appointed by the pastor to serve the un-expired term.

Section 5.09—Installation Of Officers

A public installation service in which all newly elected officers of the church are to be dedicated to their respective offices and the ordination of newly elected deacons shall be held at a public church service following their election at the annual church administration meeting.

ARTICLE 6 – MEETINGS[17]

Section 6.01—Meetings For Worship

Unless otherwise determined by the pastor, the church shall meet each Sunday for public worship both morning and evening and at least once during the week for Bible study and prayer. Except when circumstances forbid it, the ordinance of the Lord's Supper shall be observed on the first Sunday evening of each month.

Section 6.02—Meetings For church Administration

(A)   The annual church administration meeting shall be held on _____, at which time the regular church administration shall be considered. A quorum shall consist of the members present.

(B)   All church administration meetings shall be opened and closed with prayer for divine guidance and blessing.

(C)   The moderator shall determine the rules of procedure according to his sense of fairness and common sense, giving all members a reasonable opportunity to be heard on a matter. The moderator is the final authority on questions of procedure, and his decision is final and controlling. The following order shall be observed at the regular church administration meetings:

---

17 *Include how often and where meetings will be held, how special meetings may be called, and the procedures for notifying members of annual, regular, and special meetings. This section should also define the ministry's fiscal year. It is important that church documents carefully spell out the rules and procedures for all church administration meetings, including who is to preside at the meeting and the number of eligible voters required for a quorum. CLA strongly discourages the use of Robert's Rules of Order to govern meetings because they are too specific and inflexible. Entire college courses are taught on the procedures contained in Robert's Rules of Order. We are familiar with court cases in which the issue is whether the organization complied with correct procedure as outlined in Robert's Rules of Order. It is much preferable to create your own workable rules based upon the Bible and common sense. Most organizations do not properly comply with the Rules of Order anyway.*

1. Devotions & prayer
2. Reading of minutes
3. Reception of members
4. Dismissal of members
5. Report of officers
6. Reports of standing committees
7. Reports of special committees
8. Unfinished matters
9. Election of officers
10. New matters
11. Adjournment
12. Benediction

(D)   For any meeting under this article, the moderator, in his sole discretion, shall have full and unilateral authority to require nonmembers to leave the meeting room and to order the immediate removal of any member or other person present who is deemed by the moderator to be disruptive to the proceedings by act or presence. The moderator shall have full authority to order the removal of all children (ages to be determined by the moderator) if the moderator determines, in his sole discretion, that circumstances so warrant. If the moderator determines that compliance with his order of removal is unsatisfactory, the moderator may, in his sole discretion, revoke the disruptive person's right to remain on the premises in accordance with Section 3.03(C) and treat the person as a trespasser.

Section 6.03—Special Meetings

(A)   The pastor (or deacons if the office of pastor is vacant or the pastor is the subject of possible disciplinary action) may call a special meeting by giving notice of such a meeting and the purpose for which it is called to the church from the pulpit at least one Sunday and not less than one week prior to said meeting. A meeting for the calling of a pastor or the severance of the relationship between the church and pastor shall be called in accordance with the provision of Section 4.04(A).

(B)   Bible conferences, missionary conferences, and revivals may be held as the pastor deems beneficial.

Section 6.04—Fiscal Year

The fiscal year of the church shall begin January 1st and end December 31st.

ARTICLE 7 – MINISTRY OF EDUCATION

Section 7.01—Purpose

The church believes that it is to provide the members' children with an education which is based upon and consistent with Biblical teachings. The church believes that the home and church are responsible before God for providing a Christian education. To this end, the church shall engage in ministries in education in keeping with the following dictates.

Section 7.02—church Participation

All educational programs or courses of instruction formulated and offered by the church shall be primarily for the benefit of the members of the church; however, the pastor may permit nonchurch members to participate in church educational programs or courses of instruction if he deems it in the best interest of the church.

Section 7.03—Staff Membership

All instructors, teachers, and administrators shall be members of this church.   This provision shall not apply to visiting missionaries, evangelists, or preachers engaged for the purpose of delivering sermons, conducting revivals, or other special meetings on a temporary basis.

Section 7.04—Statement of Faith Accord

All educational programs or courses of instruction shall be taught and presented in full accord with the Statement of Faith of the church.

The church shall not hire, appoint, or retain any employee or volunteer for its educational programs who fails to adhere to or expresses disagreement with the Statement of Faith.

Section 7.05—Unity

All educational programs or courses of instruction shall be conducted as an integral and inseparable ministry of the church.

Section 7.06—Teaching

All educational programs or courses of instruction shall be conducted consistent with the teaching of the inerrant Word of God. Any assertion or belief which conflicts with or questions a Bible truth is a pagan deception and distortion of the truth which will be disclaimed as false. It is the responsibility of every instructor or teacher to present the inerrant Word of God as the sole infallible source of knowledge and wisdom.

Section 7.07—Christian Walk

All administrators, instructors, and teachers shall continue or adopt a lifestyle consistent with the precepts which they teach, whether in or out of the classroom.

ARTICLE 8 – ORDINATION[18]

Section 8.01—Ordination Qualifications

Any member of this church or its mission churches, who gives evidence of a genuine call of God into the work of the ministry and possesses the qualifications stated in 1 Timothy 3:1-7 and Titus 1:6-9, may be ordained as a minister of the Gospel.

Section 8.02—Ordination Procedure

---

18 *The bylaws should set forth the qualifications for a candidate for licensing or ordination and should direct who will determine whether the candidate should be presented to the church for licensing or ordination.*

(A)   Upon a conference with the pastor and after the pastor has approved the candidate for ordination, the pastor shall call a council to examine and pass on the qualification of the candidate. The ordination council shall consist of ordained ministers of like faith invited to participate in the examination of the candidate.

(B)   If the candidate is found worthy of ordination by the council, the ordination council may ordain the candidate on behalf of the church.

(C)   The pastor and the chairman of the deacons shall arrange for the ordination service.

ARTICLE 9 – INDEMNIFICATION[19]

Section 9.01—Actions Subject To Indemnification20

The church may indemnify any person who was or is a party or is threatened to be made a party to any threatened, pending or completed action, suit, or proceeding, whether civil, criminal, administrative, or

---

19 *Indemnification is an important protection for those in authority in the church. It assures the officers that the church is willing to back their good-faith decisions on behalf of the church. Indemnification simply means that the church is able to pay for the defense or any damage that occurs when an officer makes a decision for which he is later sued. We suggest that indemnification be subject to the approval of the deacons or other authority so that the church has the option of indemnification.*

20 *If a staff member or volunteer of the church is sued because of his connection with the church, a church may decide to reimburse him for expenses he incurs in defending that legal action. The church staff member or volunteer is entitled to the reimbursement only if he believed he was acting in the best interests of the church and in a lawful manner when he performed the actions for which he is being sued. The fact that he loses the legal action does not necessarily mean that he did not perform his duties with the best interests of the church in mind or that he knew his actions were unlawful. Even if he loses the legal action, the church staff member or volunteer could still be entitled to reimbursement if he acted in what he believed to be the church's best interests and in a lawful manner.*

investigative, including all appeals (other than an action by or in the right of the church) by reason of the fact that the person is or was a pastor, deacon, officer, employee, or agent of the church, against expenses, including attorneys' fees, judgments, fines, and amounts paid in settlement actually and reasonably incurred by him in connection with the action, suit, or proceeding; and if that person acted in good faith and in a manner he reasonably believed to be in or not opposed to the best interests of the church and, with respect to any criminal action or proceeding, had no reasonable cause to believe his conduct was unlawful. The termination of any action, suit, or proceeding by judgment, order, settlement, conviction, or on a plea of *nolo contendere* or its equivalent, shall not, of itself, create a presumption that the person did not act in good faith and in a manner that he reasonably believed to be in or not opposed to the best interests of the church and, with respect to any criminal action or proceeding, had no reasonable cause to believe that his or her conduct was unlawful.

Section 9.02—Expenses Subject To Indemnification

To the extent that a pastor, deacon, officer, employee, or agent has been successful on the merits or otherwise in defense of any action, suit, or proceeding referred to in this Article, or in defense of any claim, issue, or matter in that action, suit, or proceeding, he or she may be indemnified against expenses, including attorneys' fees, actually and reasonably incurred by him or her in connection with the action, suit, or proceeding.[21]

Section 9.03—Limitations Of Indemnification[22]

------

21 *If the staff member or volunteer of the church is successful in defending the legal action against him, he may be reimbursed for expenses actually and reasonably incurred by him in connection with that legal action. This means the expenses may not be unreasonably high for a legal action of the type in which he is involved. Attorneys' fees are considered to be an expense for which the staff member or volunteer may be reimbursed.*

22 *Before the staff member or volunteer may be reimbursed, the church must determine that he is entitled to the reimbursement because he acted in what he believed to be the best interests of the church or because he acted with no knowledge that what he was doing was unlawful. The determination of whether the staff member or volunteer complied with this standard of conduct is to be made in one of three ways: (a) by a majority vote of a quorum*

Any indemnification made under this Article, may be made by the church only as authorized in the specific case on a determination that indemnification of the pastor, deacon, officer, employee, or agent is proper in the circumstances because he has met the applicable standard of conduct set forth in Section 9.01. The determination shall be made (a) by a majority vote of a quorum consisting of the pastor and deacons who were not and are not parties to or threatened with the action, suit, or proceeding; (b) if the described quorum is not obtainable or if a majority vote of a quorum of disinterested deacons so directs, by independent legal counsel in a written opinion; or (c) by a majority vote of the members of the church.

Section 9.04—Timing Of Indemnification[23]

Expenses of each person seeking indemnification under this Article, may be paid by the church as they are incurred, in advance of the final disposition of the action, suit, or proceeding, as authorized by the board of deacons in the specific case, on receipt of an undertaking by or on behalf of the pastor, deacon, officer, employee, or agent to repay the amount if it is ultimately determined that he or she is not qualified to be indemnified by the church.

Section 9.05—Extent Of Indemnification[24]

of the pastor and deacons who are not also involved in the legal action; (b) if a quorum of the pastor and deacons is not possible because they are also involved in the legal action, or if a majority of the quorum so directs, by an attorney who is not involved in the legal action will be asked to give a written legal opinion as to whether the staff member or volunteer complied with the standard of conduct; or (c) by a majority vote of the church congregation.

23 The church may choose to reimburse the staff member or volunteer for his expenses as they occur, but before the legal action is over, if the person being reimbursed agrees to repay that amount if it is ultimately determined that he is ineligible for reimbursement by the church. For instance, he may be ineligible because he actually knew that he was breaking a law when he performed the action for which he was sued. The deacons must decide whether the church will reimburse the staff member or volunteer as the expenses are incurred or whether they will be reimbursed only after the legal action is finally disposed of.

24 The church will have the discretion to reimburse or not to reimburse the staff member or volunteer, unless the church has agreed to reimburse him in

The indemnification provided by this Article shall be deemed to be discretionary unless otherwise required as a matter of law or under any agreement or provided by insurance purchased by the church, both as to action of each person seeking indemnification under this Article in his official capacity and as to action in another capacity while holding that office, and may continue as to a person who has ceased to be a pastor, deacon, officer, employee, or agent and may inure to the benefit of the heirs, executors, and administrators of that person.

Section 9.06—Insurance[25]

The church may purchase and maintain insurance on behalf of any person who is or was a pastor, deacon, officer, employee, or agent of the church against any liability asserted against him and incurred by him in that capacity, or arising out of his status in that capacity, whether or not the church would have the power to indemnify him against liability under the provisions of this Article.

ARTICLE 10 – COMMITTEES[26]

Section 10.01—Standing Committees

---

any other agreement, including an insurance agreement purchased by the church. The church has the discretion to reimburse whether the person was sued in his official capacity or in any other capacity while he was holding that office. For instance, whether the pastor is sued in his official capacity as Pastor John Smith or in his private, individual capacity as John Smith for his actions connected with the church, the church may decide to reimburse him in both capacities. If he is removed from his duties, or if he passes away during the course of the legal action against him, the church may decide to continue to reimburse him—or his heirs—for expenses in defending the actions brought against him.

25 The church may decide to purchase an insurance policy to pay for the defense of church staff members or volunteers and for the payment of any judgment against him for his actions on behalf of the church.

26 Committees should be flexible in the bylaws. The church should not list all committees in the bylaws, but should retain the authority to create and dissolve committees as it chooses. Most committees are temporary and should be treated in the bylaws as such.

The pastor (or the board of deacons if the office of pastor is vacant) shall appoint standing committees and designate a chairperson for each standing committee and, except when otherwise specifically provided in these bylaws, shall determine the membership of each standing committee. In addition to the discipline committee, the pastor may appoint other standing committees as he deems appropriate.

Section 10.02—Special Committees
The board of deacons, in its discretion, may create special committees to provide the board with advice and information regarding matters submitted to the committee by the board for consideration. The committee shall have no authority to act on behalf of the corporation. The members of the committee shall be chosen by a majority vote of the board of deacons and shall serve solely at the pleasure of the board of deacons. The special committee shall be subject to the control and direction of the board of deacons at all times.

ARTICLE 11 – DESIGNATED CONTRIBUTIONS[27]

From time to time the church, in the exercise of its religious, educational, and charitable purposes, may establish various funds to accomplish specific goals. Contributors may suggest uses for their contributions, but all suggestions shall be deemed advisory rather than mandatory in nature. All contributions made to specific funds or otherwise designated shall remain subject to the exclusive control and discretion of the pastor and the board of deacons. No fiduciary obligation shall be created by any designated contribution made to the church other than to use the contribution for the general furtherance of any of the purposes

---

27 *Contributions that are designated by the contributor for a specific purpose impose a "trust" obligation upon the recipient church to use the designated funds for that purpose only. For example, if a designation is made for the building fund, the amount designated must be used solely for the purpose of that building fund. If the church receives a designated contribution, there are only three things the church may legally do with the money: use it for the purpose designated, return the gift to the donor, or have the donor change or remove the designation. To avoid being required to ask the donor for permission to use the funds for a purpose other than the designated purpose, the bylaws should contain a specific provision making gift designation advisory only.*

stated in Section 1.02.

ARTICLE 12 – BINDING ARBITRATION[28]

Section 12.01—Submission To Arbitration

Believing that lawsuits between believers are prohibited by Scripture, all members of this church agree to submit to binding arbitration any matters which cannot otherwise be resolved, and expressly waive any and all rights in law and equity to bringing any civil disagreement before a court of law, except that judgment upon the award rendered by the arbitrator may be entered in any court having jurisdiction thereof.

Section 12.02—Notice Of Arbitration

In the event of any dispute, claim, question, or disagreement arising out of or relating to these bylaws or any other church matter, the parties shall use their best efforts to settle such disputes, claims, questions, or disagreement as befits Christians. To this effect, they shall consult and negotiate with each other in good faith and, recognizing their mutual interests not to disgrace the name of Christ, seek to reach a just and equitable solution. If they do not reach such solution within a period of sixty (60) days, then upon notice by either party to the other, disputes, claims, questions, or differences shall be finally settled by arbitration as described in Section 12.01, above, and such Procedures for Arbitration as are adopted pursuant to Section 12.04, below.

Section 12.03—Limitations On Arbitration Decisions

(A)   Should any dispute involve matters of church discipline, the arbitrators shall be limited to determining whether the procedures for church discipline as outlined under Section

---

28 *Make sure that your bylaws provide that any and all disputes between a church member and the church cannot be litigated in the civil courts as this is Biblically forbidden, but, if such a dispute does arise, that the matter would be arbitrated in a Biblically based Christian manner. We recommend that you not use just any secular arbitration procedure. Instead, we have provided a sample procedure in this resource. Following the procedures provided at Exhibit 3 will insure that the dispute is handled in a Scriptural manner.*

3.04, were followed.

(B)   Should any dispute involve the removal from office of the pastor or any church officer, the arbitrators shall be limited to determining whether the procedures set forth in Sections 4.04 or 5.06 were followed.

Section 12.04—Arbitration Procedures

The Procedures for Arbitration shall be as adopted by the pastor and the board of deacons.

ARTICLE 13 – AMENDMENTS[29]

These bylaws may be revised or amended by a majority vote of the members present and voting at any regular church administration meeting, provided that said revision or amendment has been submitted in writing and announced from the pulpit fourteen (14) days before the vote is taken.

ADOPTION

These bylaws were adopted by a two-thirds majority vote of the members present and voting at a duly called meeting of the church in which a quorum was present.

These bylaws supersede any other bylaws of _____
_____ church.

Date: _____

Minister of Records: _____

EXHIBITS

---

29 *We recommend that churches make the amendment process simple because circumstances may arise which create a need to change the church bylaws. A simple amendment process leaves the church with the necessary flexibility to address new concerns and developments. The church bylaws should address when the church bylaws may be amended, who may vote to amend the church bylaws, and what type of majority is necessary for the adoption of the amendment (simple majority, two-thirds, or three-fourths).*

Exhibit 1: Essential Tax-Exempt Provisions for Unincorporated Churches
Exhibit 2: Alternate Provisions for Churches Operating a Christian
Day School
Exhibit 3: Sample Procedures for Arbitration

EXHIBIT 1

Essential Tax-Exempt Provisions for Unincorporated Churches

ARTICLE 13 – TAX EXEMPT PROVISIONS[30]

Section 13.01—Private Inurement

No part of the net earnings of the church shall inure to the benefit
of or be distributable to its members, trustees, officers, or other private

---

30 *If the church is unincorporated, it should insert the following provisions
as Article 13 and renumber the Article entitled "Amendments" in the Sample
Bylaws as Article 14.*
*Verify that the church constitution contains no provisions which are so broad
in scope that they jeopardize the church's tax-exempt status. Be certain that
no provisions violate the requirements of IRS § 501(c)(3) requirements. IRS §
501(c)(3) provides that to be tax-exempt an organization must be:*
> [O]rganized and operated exclusively for religious, charitable,
> scientific, testing, for public safety, literary, or educational
> purposes, . . . no part of the net earnings of which inures to
> the benefit of any private shareholder or individual, no sub-
> stantial part of the activities of which is carrying on propa-
> ganda, or otherwise attempting, to influence legislation (ex-
> cept as otherwise provided in subsection H) and which does
> not participate in, or intervene in (including the publishing or
> distributing of statements) any political campaign on behalf
> of (or in opposition to) any candidate for public office.
*Therefore, to protect against loss of the tax-exempt status of the church, this
section should include provisions dealing with such matters as private inurement, political involvement, dissolution, and racial nondiscrimination.*
*If your church is incorporated, you should check your Articles of Incorpora-
tion to ensure that the following provisions are included therein. If these
provisions are not included in your Articles of Incorporation, we strongly recommend that you amend your Articles of Incorporation to include these provisions. Please call the Christian Law Association at (727) 399-8300 with any
questions about amending your Articles of Incorporation.*

persons, except that the church shall be authorized and empowered to pay reasonable compensation for the services rendered and to make payments and distributions in furtherance of the purposes set forth in Section 1.02 hereof.

Section 13.02—Political Involvement

No substantial part of the activities of the church shall be the carrying on of propaganda or otherwise attempting to influence legislation. The church shall not participate in, or intervene in (including the publishing or distribution of statements) any political campaign on behalf of any candidate for public office.

Section 13.03—Dissolution

Upon the dissolution of the church, the trustees shall, after paying or making provision for payment of all the liabilities of the church, dispose of all of the assets of the church to such organization or organizations formed and operated exclusively for religious purposes as shall at the time qualify as an exempt organization or organizations under Section 501(c)(3) of the Internal Revenue Code of 1986 (or the corresponding provision of any future United States Internal Revenue Law), as the trustees shall determine. Assets may be distributed only to tax-exempt organizations which agree with the church's Statement of Faith.

Section 13.04—Racial Nondiscrimination

The church shall have a racially nondiscriminatory policy and, therefore, shall not discriminate against members, applicants, students, and others on the basis of race, color, or national or ethnic origin.

Section 13.05—Limitation Of Activities

Notwithstanding any other provision of these bylaws, the church shall not, except to an insubstantial degree, engage in any activities or exercise any powers that are not in furtherance of the purposes stated in Section 1.02.

EXHIBIT 2

Alternate Provisions for Churches Operating a Christian Day School

ARTICLE 7 – MINISTRY OF EDUCATION[31]

Section 7.1—Purpose

The church believes that it is to provide the members' children with an education which is based upon and consistent with Biblical teachings. The church believes that the home and church are responsible before God for providing a Christian education. In order to assist the church's families with their obligation to Biblically train their children, the church shall operate a Christian day school. To this end, the church shall engage in ministries in education in keeping with the following dictates.

Section 7.2—Church Participation

All educational programs or courses of instruction formulated and offered by the church shall be primarily for the benefit of the members of the church; however, the pastor may permit nonchurch members to participate and enroll their children in the church's educational programs or courses of instruction if he deems it in the best interest of the church.

Section 7.3—Staff Membership

All instructors, teachers, and administrators shall be members of this church. This provision shall not apply to visiting missionaries, evangelists, or preachers engaged for the purpose of delivering sermons, conducting revivals, or other special meetings on a temporary basis.

Section 7.4—Statement of Faith Accord

All educational programs or courses of instruction shall be taught and presented in full accord with the Statement of Faith of the church.

---

31 *If your ministry has a Christian day school or daycare ministry, we recommend that the following be substituted for the Article 7 included in the Sample Bylaws.*

The church shall not hire, appoint, or retain any employee or volunteer for its educational programs who fails to adhere to or expresses disagreement with the Statement of Faith.

Section 7.5—Unity

All educational programs or courses of instruction shall be conducted as an integral and inseparable ministry of the church.

Section 7.6—Teaching

All educational programs or courses of instruction shall be conducted consistent with the teaching of the inerrant Word of God. Any assertion or belief which conflicts with or questions a Bible truth is a pagan deception and distortion of the truth which will be disclaimed as false. It is the responsibility of every instructor or teacher to present the inerrant Word of God as the sole infallible source of knowledge and wisdom.

Section 7.7—Christian Walk

All administrators, instructors, teachers, and other staff, whether paid or volunteer, shall continue or adopt and maintain a lifestyle consistent with the precepts taught by the church, whether in or out of the classroom. All staff shall be under the supervision of the pastor who has the sole authority to hire, appoint, or dismiss the same as stated herein.

Section 7.8—Hierarchy of Authority

(A)   The pastor shall be the final authority on all matters relating to the ministry of education. The pastor shall have the authority to approve or disapprove any decision or recommendation of the board of deacons on all matters relating to the ministry of education.

       1.   Subject to the approval of the church membership and on the condition that they shall become a member of the church upon assuming duties, the pastor may hire administrators and principals to assist the pastor in carrying out the ministry of education.

2. On the condition that they shall become a member of the church upon assuming duties, the pastor may hire teachers and support staff to assist the pastor in carrying out the ministry of education.

(B) The board of deacons shall assist and advise the pastor on all matters relating to the ministry of education. The board of deacons shall act as the school board and shall hear all matters and disputes which may arise out of the ministry of education and shall advise the pastor accordingly. All recommendations of the board of deacons shall be submitted to the pastor for final approval prior to becoming effective. The board of deacons may create and recommend to the pastor school policies for governing the ministry of education consistent with the provisions herein.

EXHIBIT 3

Sample Procedures for Arbitration

PROCEDURES FOR ARBITRATION[32]

Section 1—Scope of ARBITRATION

The parties must, prior to the selection of arbitrators, agree to the scope of the matters to be considered by the arbitrators. In doing so the parties must conduct themselves with the utmost courtesy as befits believers in Jesus Christ. If the parties cannot agree upon the scope of the dispute for arbitration, the scope shall be determined by the arbitrators.

---

32 *Our Sample Bylaws call for the pastor and board of deacons to adopt procedures for arbitration. Accordingly, we recommend that these procedures be adopted as soon as possible. Since these procedures are not a part of the bylaws, they are not required to be voted upon by the church members and should not be included in the church bylaws. These procedures should be attached to the minutes of the board of deacons meeting in which they are adopted, and should be kept in a safe place with the other important church documents.*

Section 2—Submission to Arbitration

(A)   The parties, as Christians, believing that lawsuits between Christians are prohibited by Scripture, and having agreed, according to Article 12 of the church bylaws, to submit disputes to binding arbitration, and to waive any legal right to take the dispute to a court of law, will refer and submit any and all disputes, differences, and controversies whatsoever within the agreed scope of arbitration to a panel of three arbitrators, to be selected as follows:

1.   All arbitrators must be born-again Christians of good reputation in the community and who affirm the church's Statement of Faith in its entirety.

2.   Each party shall submit a list of three proposed arbitrators to the other party, and the other party will choose one of the three proposed arbitrators to serve on the panel.

3.   The third arbitrator will be selected by mutual agreement of the other two arbitrators.

4.   In selecting the arbitrators, each party shall act in good faith in choosing Christian arbitrators who have no prior knowledge of the facts leading up to the dispute, are not related to or close friends with the selecting party, and who will act impartially and with fundamental fairness.

5.   No arbitrator may be an attorney.

6.   No arbitrator may be employed or ever have been employed by, or under the authority of, either party or any other arbitrator.

7.   The arbitrators will be selected as soon as possible but no later than 30 days after the parties have agreed to the scope of the arbitration.

8.   The arbitration will be held at a neutral site agreed to by the arbitrators.

(B)   The arbitrators shall, subject to the provisions of these procedures, arbitrate the dispute according to the terms of these procedures, the Bible as interpreted by the church's Statement of Faith, and any applicable church documents.

(C)   Each party may be represented by counsel throughout the process at the party's own expense. Discovery will be allowed as needed, as determined in the discretion of the arbitrators. Formal rules of evidence shall not apply.

Section 3—Terms and Conditions of Arbitration

(A)   The arbitrators shall have full power to make such regulations and to give such orders and directions, as they shall deem expedient in respect to a determination of the matters and differences referred to them.

(B)   The arbitrators shall hold the arbitration hearing as soon as possible, but no later than thirty (30) days after the selection of the third arbitrator.

(C)   There shall be no stenographic record of the proceedings, and all proceedings shall be closed to the media and any other individuals not directly involved in the proceedings.

(D)   Normally, the hearing shall be completed within three (3) hours. The length of the hearing, however, may be extended by the arbitrators in their discretion or an additional hearing may be scheduled by the arbitrators to be held promptly.

(E)   There will be no post-hearing briefs.

(F)   The arbitrators are to make and publish their award, in writing, signed by each of them concerning the matters referred, to be delivered to the parties no later than 48 hours from the conclusion of the hearing, unless otherwise agreed by the parties. The arbitrators may, in their discretion, furnish an opinion.

Section 4—Conduct and Rules of Hearing

(A) The arbitrators may, in their absolute discretion, receive and consider any evidence they deem relevant to the dispute, whether written or oral, without regard to any formal rules of evidence.

(B) The parties and their respective witnesses must, when required by the arbitrators, attend and submit to examination and cross-examination under oath as to all or any of the matters referred to in the proceedings and to produce and deposit with the arbitrators all or any evidence within their possession or control concerning such matters.

(C) If a party defaults in any respect referred to in Subsection 4(B), above, the arbitrators may proceed with the arbitration in their discretion as if no such evidence were in existence, insofar as it may be favorable to the party in default.

(D) All presentations shall be controlled by the arbitrators. Any disputes regarding procedure shall be decided solely by the arbitrators.

Section 5—Duties of Arbitrators

(A) The arbitrators are to receive all evidence, prayerfully consider such evidence in an impartial manner, and render a decision which, based upon Scriptural principles, is fair to all parties.

(B) The arbitrators have full power to order mutual releases to be executed by the parties, and either of the parties failing, such orders shall have the effect of a release, and may be duly acknowledged as such.

(C)   In the event that either party or a witness for either party shall fail to attend the arbitration hearing, after such written notice to such party as the arbitrators shall deem reasonable, the arbitrators may proceed in the absence of such party or witnesses without further notice.

Section 6—Decision of Arbitrators

(A)   It is preferred that the arbitrators reach a unanimous decision, but if a unanimous decision cannot be obtained, a majority decision will be accepted. The written decision of a majority of the arbitrators shall be final and binding on all parties, and judgment upon the award rendered by the arbitrators may be entered in any court having jurisdiction thereof. There is no appeal from the decision of the arbitrators.

(B)   The decision of the arbitrators is to be kept confidential by all parties for a period of one year. For purposes of these procedures, the church membership may be informed of the decision if the church or any church pastors, officers, trustees, employees, or board members were a party to the proceeding.

(C)   Should any party commence legal proceedings against another party with respect to the agreed scope of the dispute or the binding decision of the arbitrators, with the exception of an action to enforce the decision of the arbitrators, that party shall pay to the other party all expenses of said proceedings, including reasonable attorneys' fees. In the event it becomes necessary for one party to commence legal proceedings to enforce the decision of the arbitrators, the non-prevailing party must bear all of the costs of said proceedings, including reasonable attorneys' fees.

Section 7—Parties to Cooperate

No party shall unreasonably delay or otherwise prevent or impede the arbitration proceedings. No party will involve the news media in the dispute in any way. No party shall publicize the dispute in any way to anyone not a party to the proceedings, except as permitted by the arbitrators and except that a party may disclose the proceedings of this arbitration to his or her spouse, legal counsel, accountants, insurance carrier, and as otherwise required by law.

Section 8—Costs and Expenses

Each party shall pay his or her own costs and expenses related to presenting the party's case to the arbitrators. The costs of the arbitration, including any fees for the arbitrators is to be shared equally by both parties.

Section 9—Amendments

These Procedures for Arbitration may be revised or amended by a majority vote of the board of deacons present and voting at any regular board meeting.

Section 10—Adoption

(A)   These Procedures for Arbitration were adopted by a majority vote of the board of deacons at which a quorum was present.

(B)   These Procedures for Arbitration supersede any other Procedures for Arbitration previously adopted by the board of deacons, if any exist.

_____

Date Approved

_____

Chairman, Board of Deacons

ABOUT THE AUTHORS

CARL HERBSTER

Dr. Carl Herbster is the senior pastor at Tri-City Ministries in Independence, Missouri. He and his wife Debbie have three sons, who, along with their wives, also serve in full-time ministry.

God used Pastor Herbster's early years in business to prepare him for a varied ministry. Tri-City also sponsors a Christian day school, a seminary, a foreign missions agency, and a Christian camp. The church has also started many churches, both locally and internationally, and Bible colleges in Mexico and Romania. Pastor Herbster is the founder of AdvanceUSA (a values action organization) and has served as president of the American Association of Christian Schools.

Dr. Herbster has a pastor's heart, a businessman's sense, a teacher's spirit, and a parent's wisdom. With this background he writes biblically and practically on the organization of the local New Testament church and how a pastor and deacons can serve together harmoniously.

KEN HOWERTON

Ken Howerton's life is all about people. He has served as a deacon and as chairman of deacons in two churches (Missouri and Tennessee). He has been a Sunday school teacher for fifth-grade boys, a bus director, and a choir member. Since his retirement from IBM, he has given his time to work with the Tri-City Baptist Missions office.

His career as a certified project manager with IBM required him to collaborate with many people to accomplish very large jobs. He also served as a Quality Assurance Manager, taught the IBM Global Service System Integration methodology in the company, and mentored professionals in IBM systems of project management.

The Howertons have also seen God's blessing in their family, with three children and eleven grandchildren.

As a man of proven integrity, insight, loyalty, and leadership, Ken Howerton shows how people serving in local churches can make a difference in their communities.

Made in the USA
Coppell, TX
06 January 2022

71119112R10136